BRACE
FOR
IMPACT

BRACE FOR IMPACT:
A Biblical Blueprint For Building Wealth And Breaking Strongholds

Learn more about the brothers at BenhamBrothers.com.

Learn more about Expert Ownership at ExpertOwnership.com.

Published in Charlotte, North Carolina, by Benham Media.

Unless otherwise indicated, Scripture quotations are taken from the Holy Bible, New International Version* and New American Standard Bible*

...New International Version*, NIV*. © 1973, 1978, 1984, 2011 by Biblica, Inc.* Used by permission of Zondervan. All rights reserved worldwide.

...New American Standard Bible*, NASB*. © 1960, 1962, 1963, 1968, 1971, 1972, 1973, 1975, 1977, 1995 by The Lockman Foundation. Used by permission.

Cover image by Larry Hubatka
Interior & cover design by Shabbir Badshah

ISBN paperback: 979-8-9893418-7-0
ISBN hardback: 979-8-9923386-0-7
Audio Book ISBN: 979-8-9893418-8-7
E-Book ISBN: 979-8-9893418-9-4

Library of Congress Control Number: 2024927289

Printed in the United States of America

Bulk purchases available. Contact through BenhamBrothers.com.

BRACE
FOR
IMPACT

**A Biblical Blueprint For Building
Wealth and Breaking Strongholds**

DAVID AND JASON BENHAM

DEDICATION

To our good friend, Joe Johnson.

You believed in us when others doubted, stood by us when others walked away, and pushed us to create when we might have settled for less. This book exists because you saw its potential before we did and insisted it had a place on your stage.

We honor you as a leader, value you as a partner, and love you as a brother.

We are forever thankful.

MORE BOOKS BY THE **BROTHERS**

WHATEVER THE COST
Facing Your Fear, Dying To Your Dreams,
And Living Powerfully

LIVING AMONG LIONS
How To Thrive Like Daniel In Today's Babylon

MIRACLE IN SHREVEPORT
A Memoir Of Baseball, Fatherhood,
And The Stadium That Launched A Dream

BOLD AND BROKEN
Becoming The Bridge Between Heaven And Earth

EXPERT OWNERSHIP
Launching Faith-Filled Entrepreneurs Into
Greater Freedom And Success

EXPERT OWNERSHIP LISTENING PRAYER JOURNAL
Get The Master's Mind On Your Life And Business

BOOKS BY **JASON** AND **HIS WIFE, TORI**

BEAUTY IN BATTLE
Winning In Marriage By Waging A War

MARRIAGE A TO Z
30 Days To Relational Transformation

Visit <u>BenhamBrothers.com/Books</u> for more information.

"In life, there are two types of people:
players and pretenders.
The Benham brothers are genuine players,
and I'm honored to call them friends.
In Brace For Impact, they equip you to use your
God-given resources with boldness and purpose.
It's the most profound insight I've heard on
building wealth for Kingdom impact."

DR. JOHN C. MAXWELL,
NY Times Best-Selling Author, Speaker, Leadership Coach

TABLE OF **CONTENTS**

AUTHOR'S NOTE 1

INTRODUCTION 8

Chapter 1 - A Kingdom Collision 20

Chapter 2 - Positioned For Impact 30

Chapter 3 - The Warrior Spirit 40

Chapter 4 - A Biblical Framework For Wealth 52

Chapter 5 - Three Aspects Of Wealth 66

Chapter 6 - The Path To Passive Income 80

Chapter 7 - The Reward Dichotomy 88

Chapter 8 - Six Steps To Financial Freedom 108

Chapter 9 - A Legacy Of Impact 124

FINAL NOTE 132

APPENDIX 142

AUTHOR'S NOTE

If you've read any of our other books, you already know we played professional baseball before jumping into the business world. I (Jason) had the privilege of playing for a far superior organization than David (*You shouldn't lie to open this book. -David*). He was with the Red Sox, and I was with the Orioles.

Back in the late '90s, while grinding it out on the dusty sandlots of the Minor Leagues, we spent countless hours thinking about life beyond baseball. Cell phones weren't a thing yet, so our deep conversations happened over pay phones in ballpark hallways and crackly locker room landlines.

Those calls weren't just about stats and standings—they were about life. We'd dream out loud about what our futures might hold when the cleats were hung up for good. We talked about raising our families in the same town, building something meaningful together, and using whatever platform God gave us to make an impact.

It was during those conversations—between long bus rides and endless batting practice—that the seeds of *Brace for Impact* were planted.

The Minor Leagues aren't exactly the ideal place to build a stable life or raise a family. So, in 2001, we hung up our cleats and moved our families to Charlotte, NC. With a couple of low-paying jobs and a head full of dreams, we started over. But one thing never wavered: our goal to work together and build something meaningful.

Interestingly, our first big idea was to launch *Benham Brothers Ministries* and use our platform as former professional athletes to share the message of Jesus. It made sense. Our pastor dad had instilled in us the importance of working for God and spreading His Word wherever life took us.

But there was another drive in us—a desire to make money. Not in a greedy or materialistic way, but more like a desire to do more. We wondered what it would be like to earn a good living and provide abundantly for our families.

But we pushed that desire aside and chose what we thought was the holier path: full-time ministry. We built a website, struck some painfully awkward poses in our baseball uniforms for promotional photos, and wrote a heartfelt support letter to raise funds. Looking back, it's hard not to cringe, but it was the only model we knew at the time.

In our minds, if you loved Jesus and wanted to tell others about Him, full-time vocational ministry *was* the path. That was the box we thought ministry had to fit into. Of course, our understanding of ministry was off—but we didn't realize that yet. We were sincere, but we were also a bit naive.

Yet, just before we mailed out our first batch of support letters, something unexpected happened. As we prayed and dedicated our plans to God, we both felt a deep conviction that this wasn't the path He had for us. Neither of us had peace about moving forward with full-time ministry in that way.

But we still had young families to provide for, and doing *something* felt better than doing nothing. That's when we made a pivot—we decided to start our own business. It wasn't flashy, and we had no guarantees of success, but we did it in faith, having no clue how it would turn out.

By God's grace and a commitment to following Biblical principles in our work, we did well. Very well.

Before we jump into the rest of that story—which you'll uncover in the chapters ahead—we need to share a foundational truth God revealed to us about our identities in the workplace during that time. This insight became the bedrock for everything we've learned about wealth, purpose, and kingdom impact. It's the reason we felt compelled to include this note upfront, and understanding it will provide the lens through which everything else in this book comes into focus.

You see, a few years into our business journey, as our company was growing and our net worth was climbing, we found ourselves wrestling with an unexpected feeling—*guilt*. We couldn't shake the thought that we weren't in "full-time ministry" and, therefore, weren't doing enough for God.

Until one morning, we stood in front of a packed room of our employees, franchisees, and contractors with our Bibles open, training them on business and wealth-building principles. I (Jason) heard God whisper in my spirit:

"Who told you that you weren't in full-time ministry?"

That question may sound odd to you, but for me, it rocked me to the core. It affected David the same way when I told him about it later that day.

As we began to think and pray about it, we discovered that our entire paradigm of *ministry* was off. We didn't realize it then, but we now know we were in full-time ministry the whole time.

We learned that *where we're placed* and *how we're paid* doesn't determine the minister. It's about passion, not position. It's about God's presence in our lives and our desire to glorify Him through our work that makes us full-time ministers right where we are.

This isn't just true about us—it's also true about you.

The devil understands a powerful truth: how you see yourself determines how you *behave* yourself. If you see yourself as just an insurance agent, a banker, a contractor, or a teacher, that's exactly how you'll behave. You'll miss the fact that, in God's eyes, you're a full-time minister right where you are. And if you don't see yourself that way, you'll never fully step into the calling God has placed on your life.

God took the scales off our eyes that morning and showed us three paradigm-shifting truths that we now teach Christian entrepreneurs and wealth-builders all over the world:

- You're a minister right where you are.

- You're on mission to bring God glory.

- Your work is worship.

When you know these truths and live them daily in your job or business, watch how God will show up and bless your socks off. You may not be blessed with financial profit, but you will certainly be blessed with spiritual peace. Best of all, you will become the person God created you to be— someone who will not gain the world and yet forfeit his/her soul.

From our paradigm-shifting moment forward, everything changed for us. We no longer operated out of guilt for not *going into* ministry but out of gratitude for *being in* ministry. Our sense of failure was replaced with fulfillment as we realized we were right where God wanted us—in the workplace, generating income and leveraging it for impact.

Fueled by our newfound identities as full-time ministers in the workplace, we pressed the gas on our entrepreneurial drives and let them ride. Soon, we found ourselves owning a family of companies—both for-profit and nonprofit—across the nation and around the globe. And we had more money than we ever thought possible.

This book tells the story.

INTRODUCTION

• ● •

"A life is not important except in the impact it has on other lives."

– Jackie Robinson

The look on their faces said it all, and it marked us forever. That poor family to whom we gave gifts on Christmas Eve in 1984 sat in their living room, stunned that another poor family (our own) would bring them presents. We'll never forget the feel of a grown man hugging us as tears of joy rolled down his cheeks.

Dad was a pastor. Mom was a part-time nurse. We grew up in one of the poorest sections of Dallas, TX. But that didn't stop our parents from showing us the value of giving to others and the sense of fulfillment that came as a result.

We had also been on the receiving end of generosity plenty of times. It wasn't a stretch for someone to show up unannounced at our door and drop off gifts for us like we did for others or hand our dad a check with a "God bless you, pastor" salutation.

Whichever side of generosity we were on, we learned early in life the power of using financial means to bless others. Our parents' example taught us that money has meaning when you use it to help those in need.

But generosity is just the beginning of what we learned. Over the years, we've discovered the transformative power of using income to create lasting impact. We've witnessed how financial resources can change a city—and even a nation. Bars have transformed into churches, abortion clinics into pregnancy centers, and movie theaters into places of hope. The common thread in all these stories? A person with the financial resources to make it happen and a determination to face the conflicts that arise as a result.

In these pages, we will demonstrate that making an impact involves more than just helping others—it also means confronting darkness. Impact occurs when two opposing forces clash. When you make your peace with God, you simultaneously declare war on the devil. If you truly want to make a meaningful difference for Christ with your life and resources, you must be prepared to encounter the inevitable conflict with evil that will ensue.

By God's grace, we've made money—lots of it—and we've seen the power of using "worldly wealth" to make a difference in people's lives. We've also experienced the backlash that's come as a result of our desire to use our income to defeat darkness and impact our city for Christ. In these pages, we'll share some of those stories.

We'll take you behind the scenes of a phone call with a TV network that was pressured to fire us because of our Biblical values. You'll witness the backlash we faced for funding an outspoken pro-life ministry. We'll share the relentless attacks endured by other wealthy individuals who chose to use their resources to challenge the evil of their day. And we'll transport you to an epic battle from centuries ago, sparked by a young man with a blue-collar job and a burning desire to stand firm in the face of evil.

Our hearts burn to help believers in the workplace create and multiply financial resources for kingdom impact. We believe God has called us to "make disciples of all nations," and one way we can do that is by using our hard-earned income to transform the world, starting with the places we live.

We didn't write these pages to teach you how to make money—you already know how to do that. And we're not here to tell you how or where to invest. We wrote this book to give you something more powerful: a Biblical framework for growing your income and leveraging it to change lives, shape culture, and make a lasting impact for Christ. This isn't just about wealth; it's about using what God has entrusted to you to advance His Kingdom and leave a legacy that matters.

This book is for those driven by a passion to create a Kingdom impact in their communities, cities, and nations and who understand the importance of generating the funds to make this possible. Chances are, you're either already that kind of person or aspire to be.

You're likely one of those generous-hearted individuals Jesus celebrated—someone eager to make a difference with the resources you've been given. You probably also want to understand what God says about money and how to generate more so you can expand your influence even further. That's what we're here to help you do.

We've had the privilege of training hundreds, possibly thousands, of believers in the workplace to use their talents, skills, and resources for kingdom impact. As we begin this journey with you, let us share one unforgettable moment that perfectly sets the stage for everything you'll discover in this book:

We stood before a packed room of entrepreneurs from across the country, all part of our rapidly growing company, the Benham Real Estate Group. On the podium in front of us were three items—the conference agenda, notes for our opening session, and a Bible.

This event marked seven years in business for us. Three years earlier, our little real estate company had grown so fast that we decided to franchise it. With hardly a clue as to what we were doing, we launched and opened fifty locations in only two years. By the time we held this conference, we had grown to 100 locations across thirty-five states.

That day's audience consisted of current and potential franchisees, their spouses, business partners, and staff members. Our goals were to:

- Educate them in our business methods.

- Equip them with the systems and tools they would need to succeed.

- Help them embark on the path to financial freedom.

- Engage them to use their resources to make an impact for God in their communities.

Our conference theme was based on Mark 8:36: "*What shall it profit a man if he gains the whole world yet forfeits his soul?*" We didn't want to train people to make money without teaching them the importance of using that money to make an impact for the Kingdom.

We'd seen too many people earn plenty of profit but not use it to help others. They achieved a version of success, yet it was without any real significance. We didn't want that for the people who had entrusted their business and financial future to our leadership.

At the end of our opening speech, we asked the crowd to do an exercise with us. We've been doing this activity for years, as it keeps those we coach centered on a vital key to business and financial success: prioritizing relationships over riches. We learned it from Psalms 90:12, which instructs, "*Teach us to number our days, that we might gain a heart of wisdom.*"

We'd like to do this exercise with you right now, right at the outset of this book, just as we did with our franchisees back then.

Imagine you're at your own funeral.

You're lying in a casket, and you can see all the people walking by, wiping tears away as they pause to remember you. Your neighbors down the street, coworkers, clients, distant relatives, close friends, and some not-so-close friends are all present to pay their respects. Then your spouse walks by, surrounded by your kids, as they hold each other and cry together.

What's going through your mind at that moment? Are you thinking …

I wish I would've made more money. If only I could've taken more meetings. I wish I would have bought a nicer car. If only I had made one more sale …

…or are you thinking …

I wish I had told my friends how much I appreciated them. I should've taken fewer meetings and made it to more of my kids' ball games. I wish I'd spent as much on date night as I did on client meetings. If only I would've used my resources for more impact. I wish I had shared my faith more …

Everything going through your mind as you lie in your casket has nothing to do with business, money, fame, or success, does it? It has everything to do with *relationships.* And the most important are your relationships with God and the people He's put around you.

Now, shift your focus to another scenario.

Imagine that you own a business in Berlin in 1942. Hitler is in charge and business is booming. One day, you're golfing with clients outside Auschwitz when you see smoke rising from an open field. You walk over the crest of green to get a closer look and see piles of shoes, mounds of glasses, books, and even hair. Then, to your horror, you see heaps of dead bodies dumped on top of each other.

At that moment, what's going through your mind? Are you thinking …

How can I increase my sales next quarter to play golf more often? I need to hurry back to the office to wrap up that project. I wonder if my assistant can book me at the Chophouse tonight …

…or are you thinking …

I can't believe this is happening. I have to do something about it! I need to leverage everything I can to help these people!

You see, there were a lot of wealthy Christians back in Hitler's time. There were even big churches with fancy services. But we're not talking about any of them today. We only remember the faithful heroes who risked everything to stand up for those who couldn't defend themselves, bold leaders who counted the cost and paid the price to stand for what was right.

Our question for you is the same one we asked our franchisees back then: *What are you going to do with the money you've made?* Will you use it to "live the good life," … or will you use it to impact your community and help those who cannot help themselves?

You see, that's why we wrote this book. This is why we held that conference. We want to see believers crush it in the workplace and increase their resources to bless people and make an impact in the world, standing for what's good and true and right in the face of evil and darkness.

On the last night of our conference, we hosted a black-tie dinner. Our theme was based on Proverbs 24:11: "*Rescue those being led away to death; hold back those staggering toward slaughter.*" It was an odd theme, for sure, but we'd seen firsthand in our business journey the power of a person with a mission that pressed beyond the simple accumulation of wealth.

After we smashed some grossly overpriced and not-so-tender fillets, we read a true story that had taken place in Nazi Germany. It told of a German man who was an eyewitness to the atrocity of the Holocaust and his account of why many Germans refused to speak up.

> "*I was a young man living in Germany during the Holocaust. I considered myself a Christian and attended a little church with my family from the time I was a small boy. We all heard about the atrocities that were happening not far from us in Auschwitz, but it was too difficult to comprehend. What could we do anyway?*
>
> "*There was a train track behind our church, and week after week, we would hear the sound of the*

whistle and the clacking of the wheels as the train passed. It never bothered us. We grew accustomed to it. One morning, we heard a noise coming from the train. It was the sound of wailing and moaning. We were shocked when we realized that there were people in those boxcars! They were being led away to death.

"Week after week, that train whistle blew, and we heard the sound of those poor Jews crying out. It was so disturbing that we devised a plan. We moved up our [church] song service so that when the train passed, we would be singing. We sang as loud as we could to drown out the cries. If, perchance, we still heard them, we just sang a little louder.

"Years have passed, and no one talks about it much anymore, but I still hear the sound of that train whistle in my sleep. I can still hear them crying out for help. God forgive me! God forgive all of us who called ourselves Christians, yet did nothing to intervene." [1]

When we finished the story, we took our franchisees back to 1942, as we did with you earlier, encouraging them to make an *impact* with their lives rather than just focus on earning an *income*.

By the time we were done, several people were visibly shaken, sitting in silence as they contemplated a life of success with no real significance. Our hearts burned as we stood in front of them. We could see the Lord stirring the hearts of those who listened. It brought us a spiritual adrenaline rush to witness people view their resources in a different light.

It was a powerful moment, but the real impact of that conference happened within. That evening, the two of us felt God whispering this message to our hearts: *This is what I made you boys for. I gave you this platform to help others make a kingdom impact with their lives.*

Since that night, this has become our mission. We are passionate about seeing good people do great things to effect change in culture for the glory of God. The book you hold in your hands is a product of that calling.

In these pages, you will learn what the Bible says about wealth and how to use it to bless your family while making a difference in the world. We'll share the three facets of wealth and how each builds upon the other. You'll discover how to create passive income so you can stop trading time for money and start using it to do what you love. We'll also give you our six-step "Grip to Drip" plan to free you from the rat race and help you experience a level of freedom you've never known before.

We shared this story and did this exercise with you at the outset because we want you to think about *why* you're interested in making money and how you can use it to make a difference in the world. Your calling in the workplace is an important one. Throughout history, God has raised influential people to effect positive change in culture. They leveraged their lives and sacred fortunes to make it happen. We want to be a part of that. The question is, do you?

We believe you do—it's why you're still here. So let's join forces and walk this journey together as we strive to become the people of influence God designed us to be—individuals driven by a burning desire to use their income to make a lasting impact. Or, as we like to say, *let's build wealth and break strongholds*!

CHAPTER ONE
A KINGDOM COLLISION

• • •

"The moment of impact proves potential for change. It has ripple effects far beyond what we can predict ...You just gotta let the colliding parts go where they may. And wait for the next collision."

– Leo in The Vow

Before we share our story and the steps we took to create wealth, and before we explore the Bible's teachings about money and how to use it to make a difference in people's lives, we need to lay a solid foundation for our time together. We'll start by defining our terms.

Voltaire once said, "If you want to converse with me, first define your terms."[2]

Satan is good at redefining words. That's how he takes over a culture. We see this happening before our eyes today, so we want to clarify our words right out of the gate.

Let's start with "Kingdom Impact." Many of us have heard the phrase spoken countless times in church, but how often do we pause to really think about what it means?

So, what is Kingdom Impact?

To understand it, we need to start with the word "kingdom." It comes from two root words: "king" and "dominion." A kingdom is a realm defined by the rule or dominion of a king.

The next question is: which king?

The answer is simple—Jesus.

It's not about King George, King Henry, Caesar, Pharaoh, or any other earthly ruler. It's solely about King Jesus and His reign.

For believers, the Kingdom is centered on Jesus and His rightful rule. He is meant to govern every aspect of our lives—our hearts, cities, nations, and, ultimately, the world. Jesus is a good king. He never forces anyone to submit to His authority; it is always a voluntary act of love and surrender.

At present, Jesus rules spiritually. But one day, when He returns, He will rule physically and visibly over all creation.

Jesus governs according to His Word—the Bible—which clearly outlines what the King expects from His people. This is why daily study of Scripture is so essential. It's not just a religious practice; it's the foundation for understanding and living under His rule. We can confidently say that the best decisions we've ever made—whether in building businesses, raising families, managing money, or making an impact— have come from consistent prayer and Bible reading. There is nothing—absolutely nothing—that surpasses the power of those two habits.

Dr. Tony Evans defines the "Kingdom of God" as *the comprehensive rule of God in every area of life.*[3]

This encompasses everything—your marriage, how you raise your kids, the policies and operations of government, the stewardship of your financial resources, how you run your business, and even how you engage with your community and culture. It includes your relationships, your work ethic, and how you use your time.

Nothing is outside the scope of God's rule. Every aspect of life, from the smallest details to the most significant global systems, is meant to align under His authority and reflect His Kingdom.

Psalm 24:1 reminds us, "*The earth is the Lord's and everything in it.*"

Imagine taking a sheet of paper and drawing a line down the middle. On the right side, you list everything God cares about and has an answer for. On the left side, you list everything He doesn't care about or have an answer for. What would you find on the left side? Absolutely nothing! God cares about everything and has a solution for it all.

As believers, this means we should be willing to engage with all areas of life. We are called to live in alignment with His Kingdom, and when we do, we actively fulfill the prayer of Christ:

"*...Thy kingdom come, Thy will be done on earth as it is in heaven.*" (Matthew 6:9-13)

How does God bring heaven to earth today? Through His people. He accomplished it through His Son, and now He continues His work through the Church—that's us. His Kingdom has already come *down* from heaven through the person of Jesus. Now, it's our responsibility to get the Kingdom *out* of us and into the world.

When we live like this—honoring King Jesus—we will have an impact.

BRACE FOR IMPACT

Now, let's take a moment to define the word impact.

Impact is *the collision of two opposing forces.*[4]

Here's the critical point: There exists another kingdom on earth that stands in opposition to the Kingdom of Heaven. It is known as the Kingdom of Darkness, ruled by Satan. We will explain in the next chapter how he came to rule that kingdom.

For now, understand this: When we live our lives with Christ as our King, we will inevitably collide with Satan's kingdom.

It's not that we *might* collide with Satan; we *will* collide with him. The Kingdom of Darkness utterly despises the Kingdom of Light. The forces of Hell are in direct opposition to the Kingdom of Heaven. As a result, they relentlessly wage war against it.

This war takes many forms. It appears as a hit piece in the local paper, attacking a Christian business owner for supporting a faith-based charity. It surfaces when a devoted leader speaks out against a city ordinance aimed at silencing pro-life sidewalk counselors. It shows itself when a generous philanthropist supports a Christian candidate who stands against the worldview promoted by mainstream media. You see it when a group of moms organize to stop the indoctrination of perversity that's taking place in grade schools all over the country.

The Kingdom of Darkness will never sit by quietly and allow the Kingdom of Light to prevail. It is constantly at war, aggressively pushing back and exerting its force against those who dare to stand up and say "Jesus is King" over all creation, including the hot-button issues.

But here's the good news: As believers, we don't fight *for* victory—we fight *from* it. Jesus assured us that the gates of hell will not prevail against the Church (God's people fully submitted to His rule).

COLLIDING AND OVERCOMING

Now that we understand the meaning of the Kingdom— the rule of God over every area of life—and that impact is the collision of two opposing forces, let's see what happens when we bring these two words together:

Kingdom Impact is the *Kingdom of Heaven colliding with and overcoming the Kingdom of Hell.*

It's not just a collision; it's an overcoming. Our role as believers is not to shrink back and avoid the collision; our role is to surge forward and overcome it.

If you avoid the collision, you forfeit the impact.

You can avoid it if you want; that's the safe route. Many churches have taken that route, backing away from conversations that desperately need truth. In doing so, they strip the warning label off the Bible and replace it with a party invitation, turning the church from a boot camp into a bounce house, making it no longer a threat to the enemy.

Satan is okay with a church just sitting there and growing because it poses no threat. He's cool with people backing out of the fight for truth and choosing to play it safe rather than risk their lives and reputations to speak it boldly. But God has called us for impact, which means there will be a collision.

THIS LITTLE LIGHT OF MINE

The problem today is not the presence of darkness—it's the absence of light! Think about it: do you have any "dark switches" in your house that turn the darkness on? Of course not! You have "light switches" that turn the light on.

When you open a closet door, does the darkness from inside the closet spill out into the room? No! The light from the room floods into the closet, driving out the darkness.

This is because darkness isn't a force or "thing" on its own—it's simply the absence of a thing. And that thing is light! If the light doesn't shine, darkness takes over. That's why Scripture repeatedly calls us to be the "Light of the world."

Our mission is clear as believers: we are called to shine our light boldly. And when we do, we should expect to collide with the darkness. But that's precisely how the light overcomes it.

Today, many of us have a skewed understanding of what it means to be the light. Growing up in the '80s, we attended Sunday School before church every week, and without fail, we'd sing the classic song *This Little Light of Mine*. Do you remember that one?

There's a verse that goes, *"This little light of mine, I'm gonna let it shine… Don't let Satan blow it out…"* It's catchy and fun, but as we've grown older, we've come to understand that the idea of Satan being able to "blow" our light out distorts the image of the kind of light we should be.

When we sing that song, the image that comes to mind of the type of light we need is a candle. A famous 90s song even told us to *"carry your candle into the darkness."* But what happens to the light of a candle when the wind blows on it? It goes out!

Today, we need to replace the image of a *candle* with that of a *coal*—like the burning ember inside a fire pit. What happens when the wind blows on it? It ignites!

Do you see the difference? The same wind that extinguishes the candle's light ignites the coal's light.

What's the difference between a candle and a coal? A candle is lit from the outside. A coal burns from the inside.

The great prophet Jeremiah said, "*Your word is like a fire shut up in my bones, and I am weary of holding it in.*" (Jeremiah 20:9)

Do you know how God gets the light that's in you out into the world? He often puts you in situations—and even around people—who will try to extinguish that light. But if you've been spending time with Him daily, nurturing the flame of His love in your heart through prayer and Bible study, their attempts to blow out your light will only serve to ignite it even brighter!

You don't have to *try* to shine your light at that moment—you just have to buckle up and let yourself burn.

When you shine your light, there will be impact—a head-on collision between the light in you and the darkness in the world.

But here's the good news: light always wins. Darkness doesn't stand a chance. That's a promise you can take to the bank (pun intended).

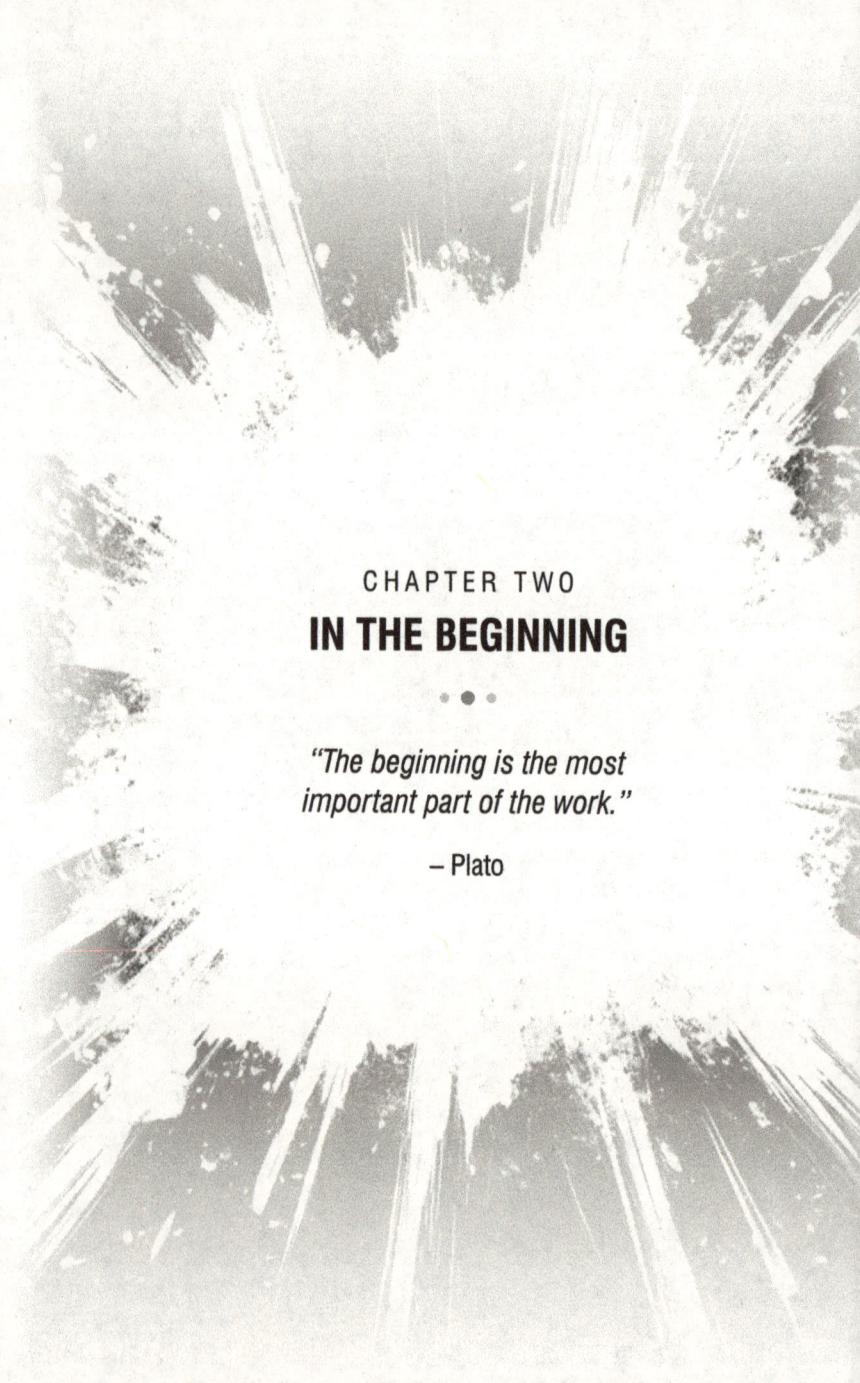

CHAPTER TWO

IN THE BEGINNING

• •

"The beginning is the most important part of the work."

– Plato

So, where did all this begin—this idea of collision? Well, let us ask you this: what was the first sin? It's a bit of a trick question. If you said Adam and Eve in your mind, that was our first thought, too. However, the first sin actually took place before Adam and Eve; it occurred in heaven when Satan desired God's throne.

Satan was once an angel in heaven named Lucifer. But pride crept into his heart, and he wanted his own kingdom, his own throne. In an act of ultimate rebellion, he dared to challenge God Himself for supremacy.

Revelation 12 tells the story of this challenge. God didn't fight Lucifer Himself—that wouldn't have been a fair fight. Instead, He instructed the Archangel Michael to do the job. Let's dive into the story:

"*Then war broke out in heaven. Michael and his angels fought against the dragon, and the dragon and his angels fought back.*" (Revelation 12:7)

How did this massive angelic battle turn out?

"*The great dragon was thrown down, that ancient serpent called the devil or Satan, who leads the whole world astray ...*" (Revelation 12:9a)

Satan ...got ...smacked! He and his angels (turned demons) got their rumps beat to a pulp.

What did God do with them?

"...*he was thrown down to the earth, and his angels were thrown down with him.*" (Revelation 12:9b)

Where did God send Satan and the demons? The Earth!

Let us ask you this: If you were God, and you created the angels with a spoken word, and then a large group of them rebelled against you, wanting to take your throne, how would you handle it? You probably would've simply spoken a word, snapped your fingers, and they would be gone. At least, that's what we would've done.

But God didn't do that in heaven. He *defeated* Satan; He didn't *destroy* him. That destruction is reserved for a future time. In the meantime, where is Satan?

He's here, on Earth.

And where are the demons?

In the exact same place—on Earth.

Did you know this battle described in Revelation 12 sets the stage for the entire Bible? You can't fully understand the Book of Genesis without grasping what happened in Revelation 12.

The opening of the Bible states, "*In the beginning, God created the heavens and the earth.*" (Genesis 1:1)

The very next verse tells us who was present:

"Now the earth was formless and void, and darkness was over the surface of the deep." (Genesis 1:2)

Darkness was present, which means that before the Earth was shaped into the ball we know today with land, oceans, plants, animals, and everything else, Satan was already there.

No sooner did Satan find himself on the earth away from God's presence, God busts onto the scene:

"...Let there be LIGHT!" (Genesis 1:3)

Genesis 1 is not simply about creation; it's about a *collision*—the Kingdom of Light colliding with and overcoming the Kingdom of Darkness!

I'm sure Satan didn't appreciate that very much, but impact always involves a collision. The Kingdom of Light confronts the Kingdom of Darkness, and when it does, it always wins.

Darkness only exists when light is turned off. As believers, our job is to turn the light on in the places of darkness, just as God did at the beginning of creation. And when we do, we can expect Satan to react, just as he did in the garden, as you'll soon see.

Back to Genesis 1. After Light entered the mix, what else did God do? He created. And on the sixth day, He reached the pinnacle of His work:

"Then God said, 'Let us make man in our image, after our likeness...'" (Genesis 1:26)

God wasn't finished with Satan by simply casting him down to the earth. He had a plan to address the rebellion once and for all. But how would He do it?

He created another being—one unlike the angels, handcrafted in His own image. God created mankind, making them "*male and female*" (Genesis 5:2).

Hold up—we can't just breeze past what's happening here. This is huge, and it deserves some real thought. Let's take a moment to dig into the key aspects of mankind's creation. There are three big things we need to look at:

- Where God placed them.

- How He made them.

- What He gave them.

Each is packed with meaning, so we need to give them the attention they deserve.

Let's begin with where God placed them.

Where did He put Adam and Eve? On Earth—the very same place where He had just cast His arch-enemy, Satan, along with his hooligan demons.

Can you imagine that? God took His cherished, innocent image-bearers and placed them in the very location where He had just confined Satan.

Would you do that with your children—put them in a place where you knew someone wanted to harm them? Not a chance! But that is precisely what God did with us (you'll see why shortly).

Second, how did God make them?

Mankind was made "*a little lower than the angels*" (Psalms 8:5). This means we carry aspects of God's nature within us, but we're not as strong or powerful as angels. Why would God create beings like Himself but weaker than the angelic ones He had already made?

We believe it's because God wanted to demonstrate what He could accomplish with the "lesser" when the lesser was fully devoted to Him than He could do with the greater when the greater was not devoted to Him.[5]

We know that's a mouthful, but read it again. Satan and the fallen angels, although more powerful than humans, could never match the strength of humanity when humanity is wholly surrendered to God. Earth became the proving ground for this reality.

You see, God wasn't content with merely defeating Satan in Heaven—He wanted to utterly humiliate him before He ultimately destroys him at the end of time.

This is why Psalm 110:1 is the most quoted Old Testament verse in the New Testament: "*The Lord says to my Lord: Sit at my right hand until I make your enemies a footstool under your feet."*

The image here shows a victorious Jesus seated on His throne beside the Father. His feet rest on the ground as He waits—for what? For Satan to be made a *footstool* for His feet.

Picture this: Satan, on all fours, crawling to where Jesus is seated, picking His feet up and resting them on his back. That's humiliation on a cosmic scale.

Here's an analogy to bring this idea home: Imagine you challenge me (Jason) to a fight, and I win. That would sting, no doubt. But imagine if, instead of fighting you myself, I said my 8-year-old daughter would handle it. Then, my little image-bearer, who shares some of my traits, wipes the floor with you. How would you feel then? You wouldn't just be defeated—you'd be *humiliated!*

Psalm 110:1 is repeated throughout the New Testament as a reminder of God's ultimate plan—to not only defeat Satan but to humiliate him completely before his final destruction.

As God's image-bearers, fully devoted to our King, we have a part to play in this. We're in the *footstool-making* business. Our role is to show Satan what God can do with the "lesser" (that's us) when we are devoted to Him than He can do with the "greater" (that's Satan) when the greater is not devoted to Him.

Is this not amazing? This is "blow-your-hair-back" type of stuff.

Now, let's dive into the third aspect of mankind's creation: What did God give them?

"...And let them have dominion over the fish of the sea and over the birds of the heavens and over the livestock and over all the earth and over every creeping thing that creeps on the earth." (Genesis 1:26)

God gave them *dominion*—He gave them authority over everything. The very thing Satan desired in heaven God now granted to Adam and Eve on Earth.

What do you think Satan wanted? He wanted that authority.

Pause for a moment. Authority and responsibility are linked. The key to maintaining your authority is to stay in your place of responsibility. Satan cannot steal your authority—you have to give it to him. How? By failing in your responsibility.

God knew that Satan would attempt to seize mankind's authority, yet we have no scripture indicating that God warned Adam or Eve that he would come for it. All we know is that God gave them a job to do and a boundary to obey.

Adam's job was to cultivate—that is, to work for a reward (more on this in chapter four). Their boundary was not to eat the fruit from one particular tree.

Isn't it interesting that boundaries existed before sin entered the world? God's blessings are always found within His boundaries.

But we all know how the story unfolds: Satan convinced Adam and Eve to cross that boundary and eat the fruit. They failed in their responsibility, and at that moment, they surrendered their authority. From that point forward in scripture, Satan is acknowledged as the *"ruler of this world."* (John 14:30)

Satan got his kingdom.

But the story doesn't end with Adam's failure—it only sets the stage for a greater victory. God sent His Son, Jesus, to Earth, and in the New Testament, He is called the "Second Adam." The Second Adam came to fix up what the first Adam messed up. He lived a sinless life, died a brutal death, and took back the authority Satan had stolen.

And here's the game-changer: Jesus didn't just reclaim that authority—He now gives it to *us!* That's right. You and I represent the Kingdom of Light in this epic clash with the Kingdom of Darkness.

We're not just spectators in this battle. We are God's ambassadors, His chosen representatives. And what does an ambassador do? They carry the rule and reign of another kingdom wherever they go.

That's our mission—to glorify God and represent His Kingdom on Earth. Every time we live out that calling, we push Satan closer to his destiny as a footstool under Christ's feet, keeping him firmly in his defeated state until the day he's ultimately destroyed.

This isn't just good news—it's life-altering, world-shaking news!

But how does money fit into all of this? We're glad you asked! To answer that question, let's turn to one of the most iconic battles of all time—a young shepherd boy, a giant, and a single, well-aimed stone.

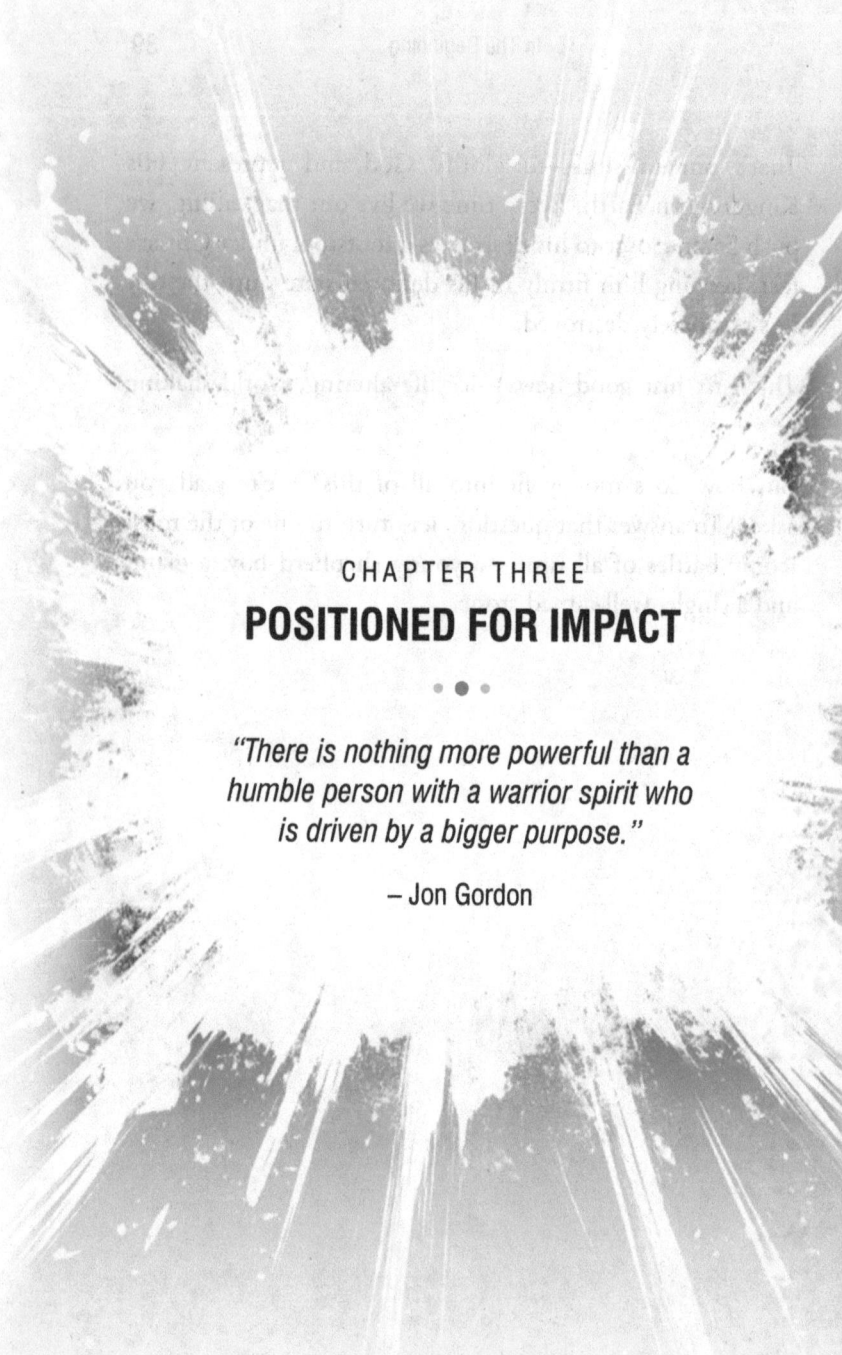

CHAPTER THREE
POSITIONED FOR IMPACT

• ● •

*"There is nothing more powerful than a
humble person with a warrior spirit who
is driven by a bigger purpose."*

– Jon Gordon

God created us to cultivate. We'll explore this idea more deeply in chapter four, but for now, understand this: God created every human being with both a need and a desire—a need to work and a desire for reward. No one wants to work for free. We *can't* work for free—we have families to provide for and responsibilities to meet.

But here's the key: our desire for reward is a good thing. Why? Because *our need for income positions us for impact*.

This truth will be a recurring theme as we move forward. The God-given drive you have to work and earn a living isn't just practical—it's purposeful. It's the very thing that positions you to make a significant difference for God's Kingdom.

And one of the clearest examples of this can be found in the story of David and Goliath.

Remember, impact is the collision of two opposing forces. Those two forces are clear in the story of David and Goliath: David represents the Kingdom of Light, while Goliath embodies the Kingdom of Darkness. As we'll see, light always overcomes darkness.

But here's something about the story you might not realize: David's job brought him to the battle in the first place. The story begins with David as a young man working as a shepherd for his father. It wasn't a glamorous or high-paying job, but David was faithful, even when no one else was watching.

Maybe you're in a similar spot right now—stuck in a job that feels like a dead end, not making the income you hoped for, or running a business that just isn't hitting its stride. If that's you, let this truth sink in: *God sees you. He cares about you. And He's at work in your situation.* Stay faithful right where you are, keep showing up, and don't grow weary in doing good. Your faithfulness in this season is laying the groundwork for what's ahead.

David's path to the battlefield wasn't paved with fame or status—it started with simple acts of faithfulness.

Back to the story: One day, his boss—his dad—gave him a new assignment. David went from shepherding sheep to DoorDash delivery guy. He was told to load his donkey with food and deliver it to his brothers, who were soldiers in the Israelite army. Little did he know that this simple act of obedience would lead to the opportunity of a lifetime.

Let's pick the story up from here.

"As David was talking with his brothers, Goliath, the Philistine champion from Gath, stepped out from his lines and shouted his usual defiance, and David heard it." (1 Samuel 17:23)

The Kingdom of Darkness always taunts the Kingdom of Light—just look at social media and most of the major news outlets, and you'll see it.

David saw the giant and heard him, but he didn't act at that moment. What was everyone else doing? The next verse tells us:

"When the Israelites saw the man, they all fled from him in great fear." (1 Samuel 17:24)

Courage isn't the absence of fear; courage is doing what's right in the face of it. They saw a giant too big to fight—David saw a giant too big to miss!

But here's where the story gets interesting—David didn't just hear the giant; he heard something else:

"Now, the Israelites had been saying, 'Do you see how this man keeps coming out? He keeps coming out to defy Israel. The king will give great wealth to the man who kills him. He'll also give him his daughter in marriage and will exempt his family from taxes in Israel.'" (1 Samuel 17:25)

David heard that a reward came with killing the giant. He would receive great wealth, become the king's son-in-law, and his family would never have to pay taxes again. Now that's enticing!

Did David ignore this? No! It got his attention. Look at how he responded:

"What will be done for the man who kills this Philistine and removes this disgrace from Israel..." (1 Samuel 17:26a)

You can almost see David freeze mid-step as his ears perk up. *"Whoa, whoa, whoa—hold up. Did I just hear 'reward'? What exactly do I get if I knock this giant dude over? Somebody run that part by me again... slowly."*

You see, the promise of a monetary reward caught his attention. Was that a bad thing? Not at all—it was a good thing. Why? Because, like us, David was hardwired with a natural desire for reward. That desire isn't some flaw to be ashamed of—it's a design feature intentionally placed in us by God. He uses that desire to position us for greater impact.

But notice what happens next. While the promise of a monetary reward got David's attention, the eternal reward ignited his passion. Look at the rest of the verse:

"…Who is this uncircumcised Philistine, that he should defy the armies of the living God?" (1 Samuel 17:26b)

David saw two things going on at the same time: an opportunity for provision and a kingdom collision. He recognized both the promise of a physical reward and the reality of a spiritual battle.

We all know David's heart—he didn't need a reward to step up and face Goliath. His courage came from his deep commitment to God's Kingdom, not the promise of payment.

But here's the thing: David didn't ignore the reward either. And the Bible makes a point to highlight this detail for a reason. Why? Because our need for income isn't separate from our purpose—it's often the very thing God uses to set us up to make a difference.

Your need for income positions you for impact.

David's job brought him to the battlefield, and when he heard about the opportunity for a reward, it fired him up. It wasn't greed—it was purpose meeting opportunity.

But here's the beauty of the story: we have no record in Scripture showing that David received all the rewards he was promised. Because that's not the moral of the story! The moral of the story is that the Kingdom of Light collided with and overcame the Kingdom of Darkness!

The giant fell, and God used an ordinary young man, faithfully working in his everyday job, with a need for income and a desire for reward, to get the job done.

Here's the key: the same spirit that drove Goliath is still at work today, along with the demonic forces that fueled him. They haven't been cast into the Lake of Fire yet—they're still active, opposing the Kingdom of Light.

But here's the incredible news: the same God who empowered David is alive and active today! And He lives in you and me. He's ready to work through you, just as He worked through young David, to make an impact right where you are.

IMPACT YOUR CITY

Let us ask you a question that harkens back to our opening chapter. If you were alive in Nazi Germany in 1942 and realized what was happening behind the scenes, what would your moral and spiritual responsibility be in that moment?

Would you ignore the fight to avoid the collision? That would be the easy thing to do, but what would God want you to do?

These were the questions swirling in our minds two years into our first business. Things were going well—we were growing, our income was on the rise, and we were faithfully supporting our church and other ministries. But then we realized a dark truth: Charlotte was a stage-three abortion-providing city. Countless moms, feeling hopeless and out of options, were flooding Charlotte to terminate the lives of their innocent babies. It was heartbreaking.

But what could we do?

We had two choices: stay on the sidelines, avoid the collision, and keep making money, or step into the fight and use our income and influence to help break down this stronghold in our city. Unsure of how to proceed, we turned to our dad for guidance.

Dad didn't believe his role as a pastor was to stand comfortably behind a pulpit, preaching to a passive audience that hung on his every word. He saw his calling as something far greater—to step into the darkest corners of our city, shine the light of Jesus, and lead his people to do the same.

Because of that conviction, our church actively ministered at local abortion clinics in Dallas. We didn't just show up;

we engaged. We welcomed moms and their babies into our church family, providing resources and support and hosting baby showers to celebrate and care for them.

Interestingly, Dad was fired for his public stand for life. His denomination deemed his stance too controversial and removed him from the pastorate. This experience became a defining lesson for us, demonstrating the courage to stand for truth, no matter the cost.

Years later, when Dad moved from Dallas to Charlotte to be closer to our family, he didn't leave his pro-life ministry behind—he carried it with him. And now, we found ourselves at a crossroads. Our business was thriving, and our income and platform were expanding, but a question loomed large: Would we have the courage to step into this darkness, join our dad in the fight, and use our resources to make a difference?

To be honest, it was a tough decision. Everything inside of us wanted to stay comfortable. But the more we prayed about it and considered the truth of what was taking place in our city, the more we knew we had to do something. So we decided that each Wednesday, we would start standing across the street from the busiest abortion facility in Charlotte and pray for that place to be closed down.

We started inviting fellow Christians from the workplace to join us in prayer. When someone expressed a desire to meet with us to talk business, we would provide the address of the abortion clinic and ask them to meet us there. Often, they would arrive and ask why we weren't meeting in our office. We told them we needed to pray for this abortion clinic to be closed down and replaced by an adoption agency first, and then we could discuss business matters.

As the group grew, we thought, *"Why not pool our resources and start directly helping these moms in need?"* So, we combined our funds and purchased a state-of-the-art mobile medical unit for a local pregnancy resource center. We parked it in front of the clinic, offering free ultrasounds to moms, giving them a chance to see their babies and receive the support they desperately needed.

The impact was undeniable—and life-changing. Moms would step off that mobile unit, clutching a sonogram image of their baby, tears streaming down their faces. A sidewalk counselor would then meet them and offer to walk alongside them through every step of their pregnancy. These counselors attended prenatal appointments, provided practical resources, connected moms with local churches, and even celebrated their courage with heartfelt baby showers.

What started as an idea became a movement. Lives were being saved, hearts were being changed, and the love of Christ was breaking through the darkest of places.

The impact kept growing, and we realized the next step was crucial: connecting these moms—who were courageously choosing life—with local churches that could provide love, support, and community. With the resources in our budget, we were able to help many of these moms directly. To expand this support, we built a network of over 60 partnering churches in Charlotte called the Life Network. This network became a lifeline, ensuring these moms had the care and encouragement they needed long after their decision.

We witnessed God move in extraordinary ways when everyday believers in the workplace stepped into this fight, using their income and influence to create real, lasting impact. But one story stands out—a moment we'll never forget.

We invited a fellow business owner to join us at the clinic one day. His name was Justin Reeder, an entrepreneur with a successful business across multiple states. As he stood there, taking in the reality of what was happening, tears began to well up and stream down his face.

"I've been in business for years," he said, his voice trembling. *"One of my best clients is right there,"* pointing his finger at the neighboring building. *"I had no idea this was happening here. I can't just walk away—I have to do something about it."*

It was a defining moment—one that would spark incredible action and ripple far beyond that day.

Over the following months, God stirred Justin's heart with a powerful vision for a national pro-life ministry. Inspired by his conviction, we partnered with him to help bring it to life. Today, that ministry is known as *Love Life*, a national movement dedicated to transforming cities by bringing the light and love of Jesus into the darkest places. Through this ministry, a culture of love and life spreads where it's needed most.[6]

As of 2025, *Love Life* has grown to partner with over 1,300 churches across 24 cities nationwide, with more joining each year. Through these efforts, over 6,200 moms have chosen life, and they've been connected directly to local churches for ongoing support and resources. And the best part of all: we've seen more than 1,000 people surrender their lives to Jesus.

But as we mentioned in the opening chapter, true Kingdom impact always sparks a collision. The kingdom of darkness doesn't sit quietly when believers step out in faith to do good—it pushes back, hard. Our pro-life stance has drawn fierce opposition, with relentless attacks and obstacles at every turn. Taking this stand hasn't been without sacrifice, and as you'll see later in this book, the cost has been significant.

Despite the challenges, we count it an honor to be part of this fight, standing as ambassadors for the Kingdom of Light and serving our great King. With Him, we have nothing to fear.

So, here's the question: What is burning in your heart? What kind of impact is God calling you to make in your city? What does He want to accomplish through you—in your family, your community, and even this nation?

God is on the move, and He's inviting you to join Him. You don't have to start a large ministry like Justin; simply be faithful where you are. When you encounter darkness in your city, don't turn away—step into it and let the light and love of Christ shine through your actions, your time, and your resources.

Embrace the collision because, without it, there can be no impact. And if that collision comes with a cost, so be it. The reward waiting for you in heaven will be worth its weight in gold!

CHAPTER FOUR

A BIBLICAL FRAMEWORK FOR WEALTH

"Run for your life from anyone who claims that money is evil. That sentence is the leper's bell of an approaching looter. "

– Ayn Rand

The church is great at teaching people how to be generous with money, but it's not so spiffy at teaching people how to *generate* it. But if we want to have a greater impact on the places we live, we better learn how.

The good news? The Bible doesn't just encourage generosity; it also provides a clear blueprint for creating wealth with which we can be generous. In the next three chapters, we'll unpack that framework and explore how to use wealth to build a legacy that matters—one that secures freedom for your family and equips you to push back the darkness with purpose.

The Bible has a lot to say about money. In fact, there are more verses on money, riches, and wealth than on any other specific topic in Scripture—over 2,300 of them![7] Clearly, God has something important to teach us about it.

But why is money such a recurring theme?

We believe it's because money represents security. That's why the phrase *financial security* is a thing. The problem, however, is that we're not meant to find our security in money; we're meant to find it in God alone. He is the one in whom we should place our faith, hope, and trust.

The danger with money is how easily it can crowd God out of the rightful place He holds in our lives. It's all too common for people to feel secure because they have plenty of money in the bank, trusting in their riches instead of the God who provides them. This misplaced trust is why Scripture addresses money so frequently—and why we should, too. If God has so much to say about it, we need to pay attention.

Let's start with a few foundational verses.

"I am the Lord your God who teaches you to profit, who leads you in the way you should go." (Isaiah 48:17)

The verse is specific: God does not *give* us profit; He *teaches* us how to make it. The word "teach" means "to train and develop skills."[8] In Hebrew, the text means, *"I am training you to develop skills."* The word "profit" means to be "valuable." Profit does not mean money in this context; it means value.[9]

Isaiah 48:17 essentially says, *"I train you as men and women of God to develop skills that make you valuable in the workplace."*

Do you know what naturally follows value? *Profit!* When you bring real value to the workplace, you earn money. At least, that's how it works in a free country with a free market. That's why it's so crucial for Christians to stay engaged civically—to help protect an environment where we can live and work according to biblical principles.

The devil despises free markets and thriving economies, especially when believers use them as tools to push back against his plans to steal, kill, and destroy.

Deuteronomy 8:18 goes even further. *"But you shall remember the Lord your God, for it is He that gives you the power to make wealth."*

Notice the verse doesn't say that God *gives* you wealth. That mindset leads to a prosperity message devoid of biblical truth. We're not here to quote "money cometh now" nonsense. God doesn't give you wealth—He gives you the ability to make it. You'll see why shortly.

Putting these two powerful verses together gives us a firm foundation to build a solid theology around wealth. God gives us the power to make wealth and teaches us how to use that power to grow it.

Before we dive deeper into Scripture, let us ask you a very important question:

Is it biblical to create wealth?

Typically, when we speak to crowds about the Biblical foundation for wealth, about half were raised to believe you shouldn't talk about money, and the other half were raised to think it's ok. There are ditches on both sides of this road. You have the poverty gospel on one side and the prosperity gospel on the other. Both of them are wrong.

On the one hand, the poverty gospel preaches that money is the "root of all evil" and that if we truly love God, then we'll be poor, just like Jesus. Of course, money isn't the root of all evil—the *love* of it is. And yes, we must be willing to be poor if God calls us to be poor. But in a country where economic opportunity is possible, there's nothing wrong with being a person who desires financial means. As you'll see later, there's a reason God wants you to grow your wealth if you have the opportunity to do it.

The ditch on the other side, however, is the prosperity gospel. It teaches that we're all supposed to be rich because God is a God of abundance. This is also untrue. If every Christian is supposed to be rewarded financially, then God needs to apologize to all the faithful believers throughout history who died without a dime to their names but are now rich in glory. Hebrews 11 lists many of them.

We don't want to fall into either of these ditches. We want to remain at the midpoint of Biblical tension and keep a proper balance. Because, as you will see, God has a plan for wealth creation in the extension of His kingdom on earth.

Let's begin our study of wealth with a definition.

Here's how we define wealth: *Financial resource that gives you options.*

Do you want options? Would you like to have financial resources to bless the people you love and make an impact?

We do. And since you're reading this book, we know you want that, too.

As we mentioned earlier, we didn't grow up with money. Our dad made 24k a year as a pastor, and our mom worked part-time at a nursing home to help make ends meet. Yet, we never felt like we lacked anything. What our parents gave us was far more valuable: a model of hard work, godliness, and contentment—a combination that shaped our lives and set us up for success.

The Apostle Paul put it best when he wrote, *"But godliness with contentment is great gain"* (1 Timothy 6:6). We saw that lived out every day in our home.

Dad taught us to rely on the Bible for everything and to put its truths into action. As he often reminded us, *"You need to turn your theology into biography, or your theology is worthless!"* If your thoughts about God don't translate into action, then what you think about God has no true value.

To show us what that looked like, he made a bold move: he relocated his ministry office from our home to a space next door to the busiest abortion clinic in Dallas. He explained, "God calls us in Scripture to stand up for those who can't stand for themselves. As a pastor, there's no better place to minister during the week than here—helping moms who feel they have no choice and speaking up for babies with no voice."

Dad didn't realize it then, but one of the employees was a woman named Norma McCorvey. She was the Jane Roe in the 1973 Roe vs. Wade Supreme Court case, which legalized abortion. Nearly twenty years later, when Dad relocated his office, he and Norma struck up a friendship that ultimately led to her salvation. Theology to biography lived out right before our watching eyes.

Dad didn't just teach us how to live out our faith; he also taught us how to study Scripture. Years later, as our business and financial portfolios increased tremendously, we saw the fruit of studying the Bible and applying it to every facet of our lives.

One key principle we discovered was the *Law of First Mention*. This principle teaches that to understand what God truly thinks about a topic, you need to go back to the first time it's mentioned in Scripture. What did it mean in that initial context? Because whatever it meant then reflects God's original intention for it.

Jesus applied this Law when he was asked about divorce in Matthew 19. He referred back to God's original intention for marriage, found in Genesis 2. If Jesus used Genesis to clarify God's intention for marriage, we can follow His example when it comes to understanding wealth.

To fully grasp what God says about wealth, we need to go back to the very beginning—before sin entered the world.

Earlier, we mentioned how God placed Adam and Eve in the Garden and gave them a job to do and a boundary to obey. In the next few chapters, we will look closer at their assignment and explore the incredible reward God had in store if they carried it out faithfully.

Let's start with the very first verse of the Bible:

"In the beginning, God created the heavens and the earth." (Genesis 1:1)

Don't just picture the globe floating in space when you think about the Earth. Instead, think about the soil—the dirt that gets under your fingernails when you dig into it.

Have you ever thought about what's inside that dirt? What God placed in the ground?

Resources.

By definition, a resource is *"a stock or supply of an asset that can be drawn on by a person or organization to function effectively."*[10]

God put assets in the ground to help us function. Isn't that nice of Him to do for us? He didn't leave us out here to fend for ourselves—He gave us tools and provisions to help us flourish. And He named them *resources* because they *reflect* the Source!

Are the assets in the ground our source? No! God is. The minute the resource becomes your source, you cease to receive the fulfillment God gave you in it because He's your source. The resource simply points to Him.

Let's dive deeper. Genesis 1 gives us the overall picture of creation. Genesis 2 gets into the details, where we'll discover some powerful truths about wealth. Follow this closely:

"Now, no shrub of the field was yet in the earth, and no plant of the field had yet sprouted..." (Genesis 2:5a)

There were assets in the ground, but they hadn't come up yet. Why?

*"...For the Lord God had not sent rain upon the earth and there was no man to **cultivate** the ground."* (Genesis 2:5b)

The resources—the assets—remained in the ground because there was no man to *cultivate* them.

What does it mean to cultivate? It means to *"acquire and develop."*[11]

God's plan was for man to dig into the dirt, acquire assets, and develop them for his use. That's what cultivation looks like.

Here's the best part—God went first! How did He create Adam? Did He speak him into existence like He did everything else in the first five days of creation? No. God did something different. He reached down, grabbed some dirt, and formed Adam from the dust of the ground. (Genesis 2:7) This act wasn't just about creation—it was a demonstration for us of what it means to cultivate.

Let's dive even deeper.

"Now a river flowed out of Eden to water the garden, and from there it divided and became four rivers." (Genesis 2:10)

One river turned into four. That's multiplication. We'll talk more about that in the next chapter. What we want to point out is the four names of these rivers and what they mean:

> Pishon - *Increase*
>
> Gishon - *Bursting*
>
> Tigris - *Rapid*
>
> Euphrates - *Fruitful* [12]

These are not words of scarcity but words of abundance! They reveal that our God is a God of overflowing fruitfulness. From the very beginning, He created a world designed for us to thrive as His image bearers.

But check out the next two verses:

*"The name of the first is Pishon. It flows around the whole land of Havilah where there is **gold**. The gold of the land is **good**..."* (Genesis 2:11-12)

The very first resource mentioned by name in the Bible is what? *Gold*. And is it described as bad? Nope—it's described as good!

God made gold before He made man.

A couple of verses later:

"Then the Lord took the man and put him into the garden of Eden to cultivate and keep it." (Genesis 2:15)

Before sin, Adam was to "acquire and develop" (to cultivate) the resources that were in the ground (including gold) to *provide* for his family and future generations and to *promote* God's kingdom agenda on the earth.

Did you catch that? Go back and read it again. And then once more. Let it sink in. This truth isn't just a passing detail—it's foundational to everything we're about to share with you about wealth.

When we apply the *Law of First Mention* to the topic of wealth, we see something powerful: the very first man was responsible for actively cultivating and stewarding the earth's resources, including gold, not just for his personal needs but also to provide for his family and further God's Kingdom purposes on Earth.

And what is God's Kingdom agenda? It's establishing His rightful rule in the human heart and His lordship over the nations. Wealth, when used properly, plays a crucial role in advancing this divine purpose.

God's original intent for wealth was clear: for man to provide for himself, his family, and future generations while promoting His agenda on Earth. This design was established long before sin ever entered the picture.

Now, think about this—when did that call stop?

It hasn't stopped! Sin simply entered the picture and perverted our motivation for getting the gold and our intention on using it. But we're still called to cultivate.

Throughout the Bible, we see people who used gold for bad and for good.

Consider Aaron, Moses' brother. He was the high priest, the full-time ministry guy. When the Israelites came out of Egypt, they had a lot of gold, and Aaron used it to craft an idol that drew people away from God.

But many years later, King David came along. He was a full-time workplace guy. He also had a lot of gold, which he used to fund the building of the temple that drew people toward God.

You see, the problem isn't the gold. It's not money or wealth. The problem is our motivation for acquiring it and our intention to use it.

As we mentioned, both sides of the wealth discussion have flawed theology. Our responsibility as believers is to avoid the extremes. We shouldn't fall into the trap of the poverty gospel, which suggests that being broke is a sign of spirituality. Likewise, we need to steer clear of the prosperity gospel, which claims that everyone should be wealthy and that lacking money indicates a lack of faith.

Instead of falling into extremes, we should find balance in Biblical teachings, recognizing that God is a God of abundance, not scarcity. He rewards our hard work with income to support our families and desires us to use that income to make a difference for His Kingdom.

Here's what you need to grasp—God created you to be a cultivator, just like Adam and Eve! He hardwired you with both a need and a desire. You have a need to work and a desire for reward. This isn't accidental; it's built into your very DNA.

Think about it: do you believe Adam dug into the ground for no reason? Of course not! He was motivated by the resources God placed there for him to obtain. This desire for reward isn't just good—it's essential. Why? Because *your need for income positions you for impact*! We saw this in the life of David before he took down the giant, and as a result, we have one of the most referenced stories in all of history.

So now the question is: how can we embrace this truth and use it to build wealth that makes an even greater impact?

In the next two chapters, we'll explore three key aspects of wealth and unpack what Scripture teaches about growing it—not just for yourself, but for God's glory and Kingdom purpose.

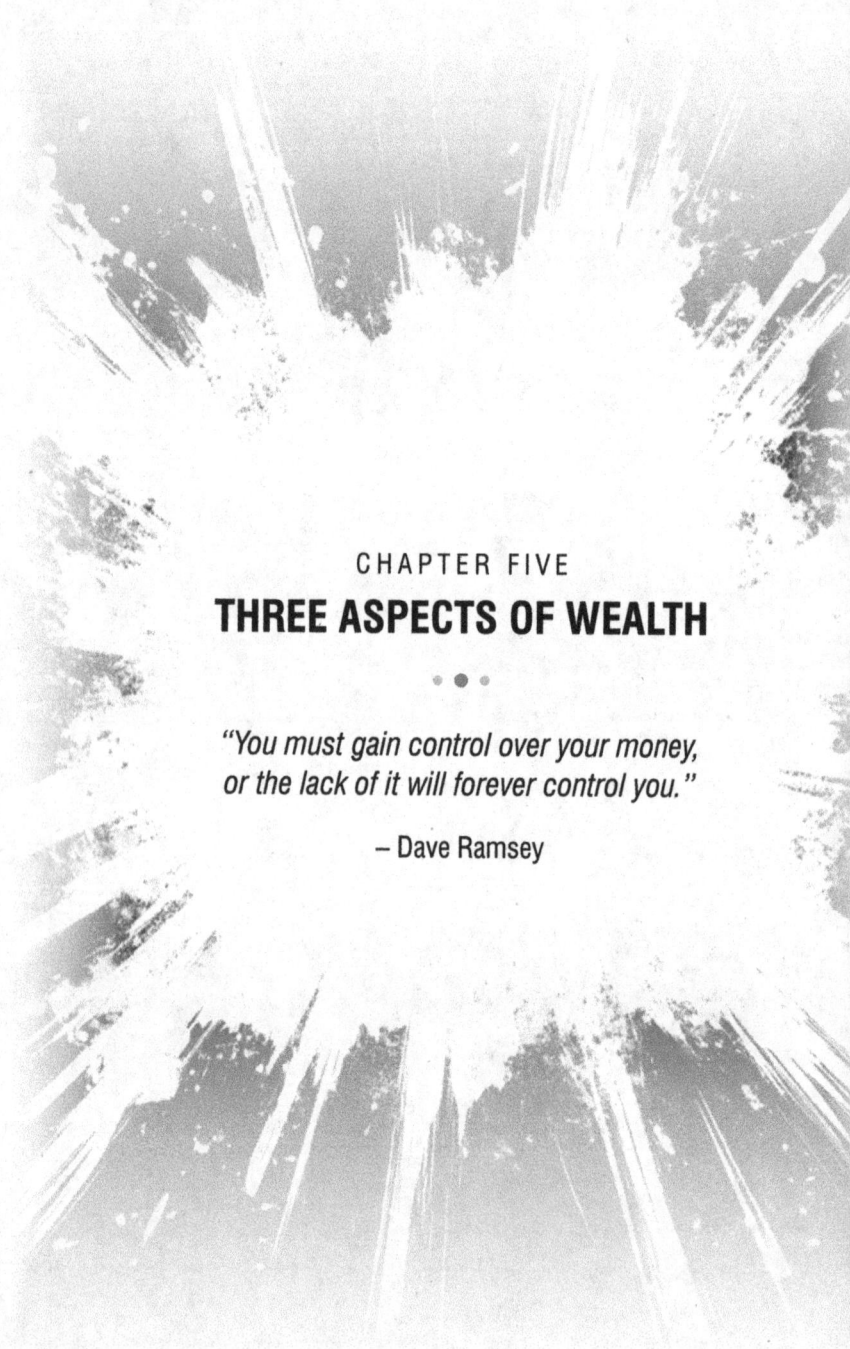

CHAPTER FIVE

THREE ASPECTS OF WEALTH

• ● •

*"You must gain control over your money,
or the lack of it will forever control you."*

– Dave Ramsey

Approaching wealth through a Biblical lens reveals not only its purpose but also its profound spiritual, moral, and practical dimensions. Far from being a mere measure of material success, wealth, when understood in the context of Scripture, becomes a test of character and a tool for advancing God's purposes in the world. In this chapter, we dive into three Biblical aspects of wealth:

- The *reason* for wealth

- The *requirement* to get it

- The *reward* when you have it

Earlier, we discussed the reason for wealth and how it ties back to Adam's original call to cultivate the garden.

The reason for wealth is two-fold: to *provide* and to *promote*.

First, you are called to provide for yourself, your family, and future generations. This is not just a good thing—it's a God-ordained responsibility.

"If anyone will not work, neither shall he eat" (2 Thessalonians 3:10).

If you have the ability to work, you must. Providing for yourself and your family is a fundamental part of your calling.

But it doesn't end there. We are not just called to provide; we are also called to promote God's Kingdom agenda on

Earth. God wants us to use the resources He gives us to bless others and further His purposes. As Solomon reminds us, *"Those who give to the poor will lack nothing"* (Proverbs 28:27).

Wealth isn't just about meeting our own needs; it's about helping others with theirs. It's about leveraging our income to make a lasting impact.

Here's the key—if impact isn't on your radar, income can easily become your idol. That's where the prosperity distortion comes in. It's all about what you'll get for yourself and your family. But income isn't God's ultimate goal—impact is.

If you focus on impact, you'll never fall in love with income. God's way of keeping us on track so that we do not fall in love with money is to use it to help others. When we operate with a generous heart to make a difference in the world, we break the chains of financial selfishness that can easily bind us.

Once we understand the reason for wealth—to *provide* and *promote*—it sets the stage for the requirement for wealth.

The requirement for wealth is one simple word: *faithfulness.*

When we were kids, our dad used to tell us, *"Boys, God didn't call you to be successful... He called you to be faithful."*

But what does faithfulness really mean? You might think of qualities like loyalty, honesty, integrity, or character—and those are all true. But when it comes to the workplace, faithfulness can be summed up in one word: *multiplication*.

In Luke 19, Jesus illustrated this concept through the parable of the talents, teaching His disciples about His future Kingdom and how to prepare for His return. While the parable emphasizes our responsibility to multiply disciples, Jesus used a financial analogy to drive the point home. How we handle money reveals the true condition of our hearts toward Him.

In the parable, a nobleman prepares to leave and receive a kingdom for himself. Before departing, he gathers ten of his servants and gives each one a talent of money, also called a mina—about three months' wages. This wasn't just a gift; it was a responsibility, and what the servants do with it will reveal their faithfulness.

Each servant received the same amount, and the nobleman instructed them, *"Do business with this until I return"* (Luke 19:13).

Notice that he didn't say, *"Enjoy this until I return"* or *"Spend this until I return."* Instead, he said, *"Do business with it—get to work, cultivate, and multiply."* Then he left.

It's pretty clear who the characters represent in this story—Jesus is the nobleman, and we are the servants.

When the nobleman got back from his trip, he *"sent for his servants to whom he had given the money, in order to find out what they had gained with it."* (Luke 19:15)

The servants lined up one by one to give the nobleman an account of what they had done with the money he had given them.

The first man said, "...*Sir, your mina has earned ten more.*" (Luke 19:16).

He 10x'd what he had been given.

The next guy said, "...*Sir, your mina has earned five more.*" (Luke 19:18).

He 5x'd what he had been given.

Is that addition or multiplication? We'd hire both guys to manage our money if they were alive today. They were multipliers of wealth.

Notice how the master responded, *"Well done, good servant! Because you have been **faithful** in a very little..."* (Luke 19:17).

Faithfulness = Multiplication.

When you operate by faith, you multiply whatever God gives you—spiritually, relationally, and financially.[13]

Notice what happened with the third guy.

He said, *"Sir, here is your mina; I have kept it laid away in a piece of cloth…"* (Luke 19:20).

This guy didn't multiply, he maintained. Why did he choose this route?

The next verse tells us, *"I was afraid…."* (Luke 19:21).

He didn't operate by faith; he operated by fear. Fear will always take you in the opposite direction God intends for you to go. Fear is like a shadow—it has no substance or power except that which we give it.

Look at how the master responded to the servant who chose to maintain rather than multiply, operating out of fear instead of faith:

"You wicked and lazy servant…" (Luke 19:22).

Multiplying requires risk. It's often scary. Stepping out in faith always is—that's why it's called *faith*. In those moments, you have to trust God.

Trust Him when it comes to sharing your faith. Trust Him when it comes to raising your kids. Trust Him when it comes to giving generously. And trust Him when it comes to investing your hard-earned money. Faith means leaning on Him in every area of your life.

As believers, we never fail. We either win or learn because our God doesn't fail. The faithful servants made their investments and trusted their master, and He was pleased.

The faithless one refused to do anything, operating out of fear, and he was upset.

Before we move on, let's examine the faithless servant more closely. Where did he hide the money? Scripture tells us he *"hid it in a napkin"* (Luke 19:20).

The napkin symbolizes the comfort zone. Every day, we choose whether to stay comfortable or step out, embrace a little discomfort, and multiply what God has given us.

The master replied to the faithless servant, *"Why then didn't you put my money on deposit so that when I came back, I could have collected it with interest?"* (Luke 19:23).

God desires gain out of his people. Why? Because that is the nature and character of God, and He is training us to be like Him!

God is a God of gain, not lack. He has not called us to maintain and just be comfy. We are to multiply all God has given us spiritually, relationally, and financially. Make your investments in these core areas of your life and watch what God does.

More is accomplished in the "pain cave" than the comfort zone.

When you know the reason for wealth—to *provide* for your family and future generations and to *promote* God's kingdom agenda on the earth—and you are committed to the requirement for wealth—*faithful multiplication* of all God has given you—it moves you into the reward of wealth.

The reward for wealth is threefold:

The first reward is *income*.

Looking back at the parable, the first two guys multiplied their starting capital by 10X and 5X. That's a pretty good income. Does God want you to make an income? Let's look to the Word.

"But if anyone does not provide for his own, and especially for those of his household, he has denied the faith and is worse than an unbeliever." (1 Timothy 5:8).

Those are some strong words right there. God takes the matter of providing for yourself and your family very seriously.

Here's another verse:

"Make it your ambition to lead a quiet life. You should mind your own business and work with your hands just as we told you so that your daily life may win the respect of outsiders and so that you will not be dependent on anybody." (1 Thessalonians 4:11-12).

God desires us to earn an income, provide for ourselves, and carry our own weight so we're not *dependent* on anyone. The devil, on the other hand, doesn't want you to be independent. He thrives on dependency, especially on systems like the government. Why? Because dependency can lead to control—and that's exactly what the enemy wants.

But when we are independent—working hard, cultivating, and multiplying—we're not beholden to anyone, we're also not a burden to anyone, and we can be a blessing to everyone. That's God's plan for you: freedom, fruitfulness, and the ability to make a difference.

The second reward of wealth is *inheritance*.

The master looked at the first two and said, *"Well done, good servant..."* (Luke 19:17).

What else does God say is good?

"A good man leaves an inheritance to his children's children." (Proverbs 13:22).

The greatest inheritance we can leave our kids is a spiritual one. That's the legacy our parents passed down to us. While they provided for our needs, they weren't in a position to leave us a significant financial inheritance. Yet, we consider ourselves incredibly wealthy because of the spiritual blessings they gave us.

Our deep love for Scripture and thirst for wisdom came directly from them, and those two gifts have been the foundation that led us to experience financial blessings. True wealth starts with a legacy of faith, and that's the kind of inheritance that lasts forever.

However, when you live in a free country like ours, and you have the opportunity to grow your wealth for future generations, you risk being like the "wicked servant" not to give your best effort. It may or may not align with God's specific plan for you, but why wouldn't you at least give it a shot?

Here's the hard truth: one reason America is in such economic turmoil is that, in just one generation, we shifted from being the world's largest-producing nation to the world's largest *consuming* nation. People have prioritized buying toys over investing in tools, and now, in 2025, we're facing a national debt at an all-time high. This is a warning sign—and a call for Christians to rethink how we approach wealth and stewardship and lead the way back for our nation.

It's time for us to shift back to being producers and start thinking multi-generationally for the sake of our children. We need to make a firm decision: our kids won't grow up watching parents who are simply maintaining. They need to see parents who are faithful in every area of life—working hard, leading by example, and committed to giving them a strong foundation and a head start in the world.

Income and inheritance, however, aren't the only rewards of wealth. There's one more reward that's far greater and much more valuable.

The third reward of wealth is *influence*.

Look at how the master responded to the faithful servants who multiplied their talents and achieved a 10X and 5X return:

"Well done, good servant. Because you have been faithful in a very little, you shall have authority over ten cities ... over five cities." (Luke 19:17 & 19).

Their faithfulness led to incredible influence. They were entrusted with entire cities and tasked with helping them flourish. This demonstrates a powerful truth: faithfulness in the small paves the way for faithfulness in the big.

In Matthew 25's version of the parable, the master replied to the faithful servants:

"Well done, good and faithful servant. You have been faithful over a little; I will set you over much. Enter the joy of your master." (Matthew 25:23).

Can you imagine the joy it must have brought those two faithful servants to receive positions of authority in cities where they could help others? They had seen the happiness it brought their master to serve in this way, and now they could do the same. It would be similar to the governor of your state appointing you as the mayor of ten cities and telling you to manage those cities just as you've managed your own home, with everyone in the local government now reporting to you.

What an amazing opportunity to bless a lot of people!

The devil doesn't want believers to have influence in their cities, and he'll do whatever it takes to stop them. One of his most subtle strategies is to shift our focus entirely to earning an income and building an inheritance—without ever considering the importance of influence. When influence isn't in view, income and inheritance can easily become idols. It becomes all about the next vacation, the bigger house, or the latest "must-have" thing. We get so caught up chasing *our* thing that we lose sight of *God's* thing—and that's exactly what the enemy wants.

Discipling the nation, as Christ commanded, falls by the wayside with this type of thinking.

Unfortunately, the same thing can easily happen in the church. It's another building, another fog machine, or some cool prop. The church can get so caught up in building its own thing that it has no real influence on the city.

So, what should we be doing in our cities—both individually and as the Church? The answer is clear: influencing it! God has called us to be salt, and as salt, we're meant to influence the places we live.

As believers, it's not enough to simply be saved; we must also be salty! Faithfulness is what gives us our saltiness.

The enemy fears nothing more than a spiritual warrior who understands how to build generational wealth and use it to influence a city for Christ. Imagine the transformation this could bring to your own city—wouldn't you love to see it happen?

The practical question is, how do we acquire wealth? How can we obtain the resources needed to increase our options?

The answer is simple: you need to turn your active income into passive income.

Bon Jovi famously sang, *"You give love a bad name,"* but when it comes to money, we need to give cash a *last name!* And that last name is *Flow!* It's not enough to have cash—you need to transform your cash into *cash flow!*

In the next chapter, we'll explore exactly how the Bible teaches us to achieve this. So get ready—it's time to take your wealth, your purpose, and your impact to the next level!

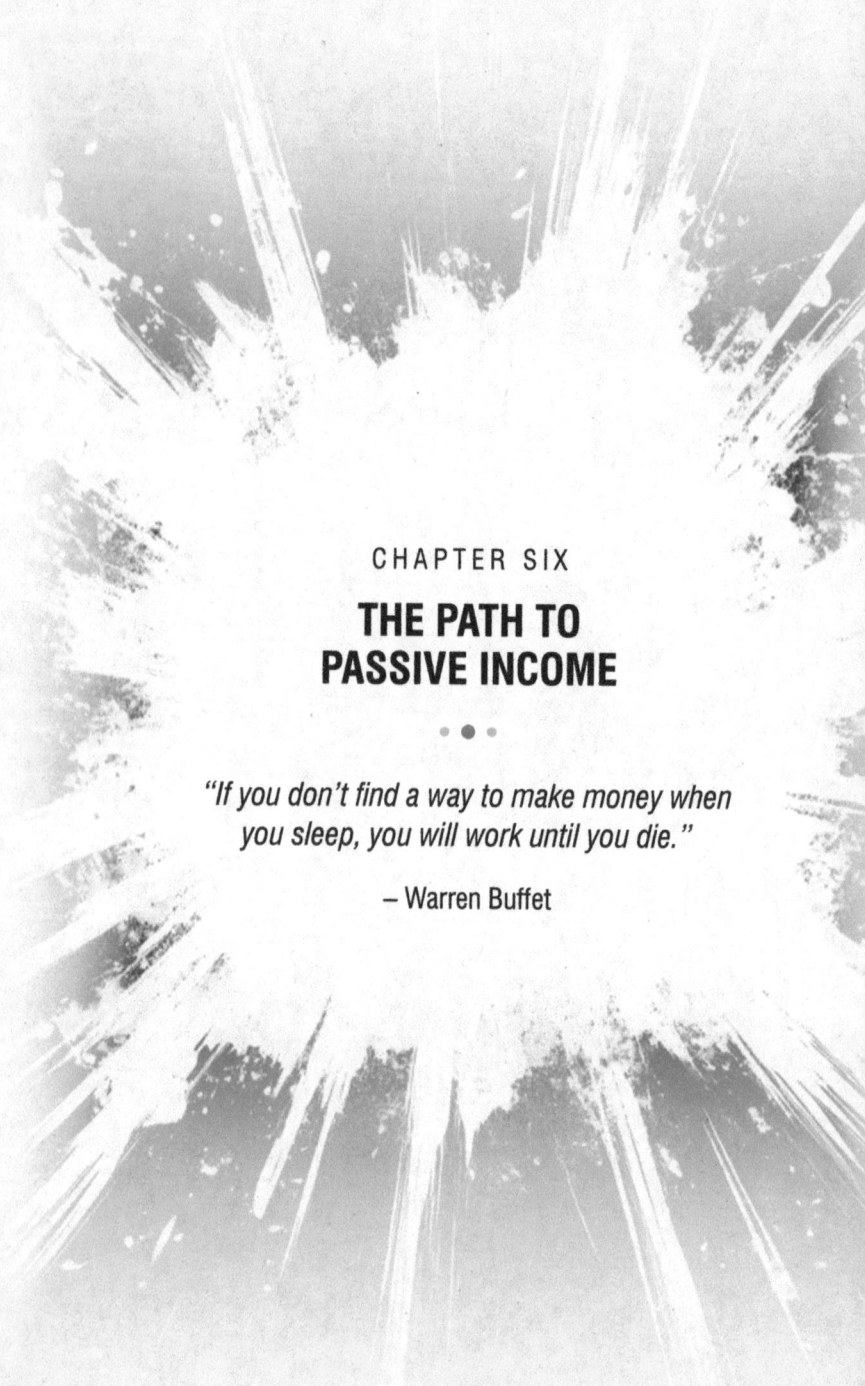

CHAPTER SIX

THE PATH TO PASSIVE INCOME

• • •

"If you don't find a way to make money when you sleep, you will work until you die."

– Warren Buffet

Did you know that Scripture makes a distinction between *riches* and *wealth*? While these words are often used interchangeably, they carry very different meanings in God's Word. Understanding this difference isn't just a financial lesson—it's a spiritual one. It shifts how we see money, use it, and, most importantly, align it with God's purpose for our lives.

Let us give you an analogy to show the difference between the two. If money is water, then riches would be like buckets of water. Wealth, on the other hand, would be a river of water. Imagine dipping a cup into a bucket of water and pulling it out. What happens to the water level in the bucket?

It goes down.

But if you take that same cup and dip it into a river, what happens to the water level?

It stays the same.

That's the difference between riches and wealth, and understanding it is key to building a lasting impact with the money you have.[14]

The bucket represents active income—your salary, hourly wage, commission, bonus, or any other form of earnings. According to our example, these are your "riches."

When you dip into that bucket to spend the riches it contains, what happens to your checking account or income? It depletes. You have less to spend on other things.

To replenish it, you have to work more. This is the classic scenario of trading your time for money—what we call active income. It's limited by how much time and energy you can give, and the moment you stop working, the bucket stops filling.

Now, think about the river, which represents wealth. The river symbolizes your passive investment income—money that works for you. When you dip into the river and spend some of its wealth, what happens to your income in the following months?

It replenishes.

And here's the best part: it happens without you having to work for it. Why? Because your money is doing the work, generating more income on its own. That's the power of true wealth—it keeps flowing, no matter what.

Which would you rather have, a bucket or a river? Active income or passive income?

It's a bit of a trick question because the answer is both! You need the bucket before you can generate the river. It starts with being excellent at the work you do to increase your active income while living below your means. That's how you lay the foundation for generating passive income and building wealth that flows like a river. We'll give you the practical details of this process in chapter eight.

Now the question is ...how do you turn buckets of limited supply into a river with continuous supply?

To explain, let us share another example:

Have you ever played Monopoly? The creators of that game probably had no idea how closely it aligns with Kingdom principles.

Think about it—what's the ultimate goal of Monopoly? Is it to just "pass go" a bunch of times and stack up cash on the sideline? No.

Every time you pass GO, you collect $200. That's your active income, filling up your bucket. And sure, it feels good to look down and see a big pile of money in front of you. But is that how you win the game? Not at all. You win the game by *owning the board!* Passive income from the properties you own and investments you make is what leads to victory, not just relying on the cash you collect along the way.

You want to own properties like Park Place, Boardwalk, and even Baltic Avenue. Then, you put single-family houses on there, hopefully upgrading to multifamily properties, so when someone lands on your space, you're collecting steady income without lifting a finger.

But don't stop there—you also want to own companies like Waterworks, the electric company, and even the railroads. Why? Because diversification leads to multiple streams of income.

This strategy isn't just a game—it's biblical. We came across this principle in Proverbs 27 early in our business journey, just as our active income began to grow and we started exploring opportunities for investing.

The book of Proverbs, largely written by King Solomon—the wisest and arguably the wealthiest man in history—is filled with insights into wealth and how to use it for good. Let's dive into some of Solomon's wisdom and see what he has to say:

"Know well the conditions of your flocks and give attention to your herds." (Proverbs 27:23).

In this verse, flocks and herds symbolize the active income you earn from work—your job where you trade time for money. Solomon's advice to *"know them well"* is a call to excellence. In other words, do your work with diligence and skill! Become so valuable in your role that your active income continues to grow and create new opportunities.

Why is this important? The next verse tells us:

"for riches do not last forever; and does a crown endure to all generations?" (Proverbs 27:24).

Your job will not last forever, nor will the "riches" that come from it. At some point, we all stop working.

The same is true for your *"crown."* In Scripture, a crown symbolizes authority—it represents the leadership role or position God has entrusted to you. Whether you're a manager, coach, teacher, or board chairman, your position carries influence and responsibility.

But that position won't last forever. Just like your job and the income you earn, leadership is temporary. The real question isn't *how long* you'll hold it but *how well* you'll steward it.

The next two verses outline a clear plan for stewarding our money faithfully and effectively.

"When the grass is gone, and the new growth appears, and the vegetation of the mountains is gathered..." (Proverbs 27:25).

This verse describes an entire year's worth of income—every paycheck, every business deal, every return on investment. It all represents God's provision over the course of a year.

What are we supposed to do with our annual income?

The next verse explains:

"The lambs will provide your clothing and the goats, the price of a field." (Proverbs 27:26).

Did you catch what Solomon did? He divided his flock into two groups—lambs and goats. The lambs were for maintaining, while the goats were for multiplying.

We're called to handle our money the same way. One portion is designated to meet our needs, providing for ourselves and our families. The other portion is meant to be invested, growing and multiplying what we've been entrusted with— just like the faithful servants in Jesus' parable of the talents.

Notice that the verse says the goats will be worth "*the price of a field*." Solomon is talking about investing in real estate—turning your active income from your work into passive income from your investments.

Whether it's real estate or another type of investment isn't the main point. What truly matters is following Solomon's wisdom: don't just earn and spend—turn your cash into *cash flow*. That's the key to building lasting financial stability and impact.

So, ask yourself: which would you rather be? The shepherd sweating it out in the field every day, trading time for money, or the owner of the field collecting lease payments from the shepherd? The choice is yours.

We all have to start with active income—it's where the journey begins. But at some point, we need to make the leap toward passive income.

Once we discovered this principle in Proverbs 27, we went all in on investing.

We committed to dividing our active income—living on one portion and investing the other. It was risky and scary, and we didn't always win, but by the time we turned 33, we were living off the river of passive income.

That didn't mean we stopped building our buckets. We kept working hard, striving to make ourselves more valuable in our careers. At the same time, we lived below our means, just as the Proverb taught us, allowing us to keep investing and growing that river of wealth.

This is what it means to turn *"theology into biography"*— taking the principles of the Bible and weaving them into the fabric of everyday life. When we do this, God is always faithful enough to show up and show off, leaving us with a testimony we can carry for the rest of our lives. That's a promise you can take to the bank.

But as we were about to learn, faithfulness doesn't always look like success in the world's eyes. God was about to teach us a lesson we would never forget—a lesson that would redefine what success truly means.

CHAPTER SEVEN

THE REWARD DICHOTOMY

*"Persecution is one of the natural
consequences of living the Christian life.
It is to the Christian what 'growing pains' are
to the growing child. No pain, no development.
No suffering, no glory. No struggle, no victory.
No persecution, no reward!"*

– Billy Graham

In chapter one, we explored our responsibility to be the light of the world and the inevitable collision with darkness that comes with it. Now, in this chapter, we'll share our story—a real-life glimpse into what happens when you use your voice and resources to make an impact in your city. What we quickly realized is that the forces of darkness aren't passive observers—they push back, and they push hard.

When you shine your light in the world, the response will vary—some people will welcome it, while others will reject it. It's like the effect of boiling water: it softens the carrot but hardens the egg. The same light that draws some people closer will cause others to turn away. That's just the nature of how it works.

In Matthew 5:16, Jesus reminds us, *"Let your light so shine before men, that they may see your good works, and glorify your Father in heaven."*

However, in John 3:20, He also warns us: *"Everyone who does evil hates the light, and will not come into the light for fear that their deeds will be exposed."*

Some may love you, and some may hate you.

This dynamic illustrates what Scripture calls a "balancing truth." It's not always one way or the other. As we let our light shine, we must be prepared for both acceptance and resistance—it's part of the calling.

In these pages, we've discussed financial success and the positive impact it can have. However, it's crucial to recognize the balance in Scripture regarding this truth. Not every good decision necessarily results in success, as we typically define it.

Here's a balancing truth we've learned: While faithfulness in your *work* can lead to promotion, faithfulness in your *walk* can lead to persecution.

Proverbs 22:29 says, *"Do you see a man skilled in his work? He will stand before KINGS. He will not stand before obscure men."* (emphasis added)

The man who's good at what he does, who's he going to stand in front of? *Kings!* In modern-day language, this means that when you're good at what you do in your work, you move up the ladder.

The balancing truth is found in the words of Jesus in Luke 21:12: *"But before all this, they will seize you and persecute you. They will hand you over to synagogues and put you in prison, and you will be brought before KINGS and governors, and all on account of My name."* (emphasis added)

The one who's faithful to follow Christ, who will he stand in front of? *Kings!* In modern-day language, following Jesus and standing for His truth will fly in the face of culture and often get you in trouble.

We call this the "reward dichotomy." Faithfulness in your *work* puts you before kings on the one hand. But faithfulness in your *walk* puts you before kings on the other.

The same faithfulness that leads to promotion in one scenario can easily lead to persecution in another.

This is exactly what happened to Peter when he preached a message of repentance after Jesus ascended into heaven. Take a look at the responses of two different crowds to the same message he delivered:

"*So those who received his word were baptized, and there were added that day about three thousand souls.*" (Acts 2:41)

"*When they heard this, they were enraged and wanted to kill them.*" (Acts 5:33)

For Peter, it was promotion from the one crowd—3k people got saved—but persecution from the other—they wanted to kill him. Yet he preached the exact same message to both crowds.

Our job isn't to chase promotion or avoid persecution but to remain faithful. God determines which path we'll walk.

After more than a decade of enjoying God's favor and promotion in business, we were about to get our first real taste of persecution.

REALITY CHECK

We started our first business in 2003 with no formal business training. But we made a promise to God: we would read the Bible cover to cover each year and apply what we learned to our business and investments.

That simple plan became the foundation of everything. By 2010, we had grown that company into 100 offices across 35 states. At the same time, we lived by the "Proverbs 27" principle regarding income—living below our means and aggressively investing the rest. By God's grace, we reached 100% financial freedom by our mid-thirties.

We could have retired then and there, but the more we prayed, the clearer it became: God didn't give us income just to sit back and relax—He gave it to us for impact. So, instead of slowing down, we hit the gas. We launched new companies in different industries while continuing to live as low as possible to maximize our investment potential.

News about our business and investment success started to spread. Then, in 2013, we received a phone call from a production company. They wanted to know if they could film a reality show about our lives and business. Little did we know that this was the beginning of a whole new chapter.

A production team came out to film our family, and before we knew it, they were pitching the footage to networks in

Los Angeles. The response was overwhelming—five different networks wanted to do a reality show about us. TLC made us our first offer. They wanted to do a show called *Twinning*. We still have no idea what that was all about because, in the middle of negotiating with them, HGTV called us.

They told us they had just signed Chip and Joanna Gaines from Waco for a one-hour pilot called *Fixer Upper*. Then they dropped the big news—they wanted to skip the pilot phase with us entirely and jump straight into six one-hour episodes of a show called *Flip It Forward*. They said they planned to feature both of our families and position us as two of the top shows on their network.

They offered us a huge amount of money, and without much hesitation, we signed letters of intent to join HGTV.

But as we soon learned, faith that isn't tested can't be trusted.

FAITH OR FEAR

By the time HGTV came knocking, everything seemed to be going great for us—until it wasn't. Long before they ever entered the picture, as our business platform grew, so did our influence. And with that influence, we openly shared our belief that God's ways aren't just best for building a business or creating wealth—His ways are best in *every* area of life, including the ones society now labels "politically incorrect." These are the very topics Christians are often pressured to avoid or stay silent about.

Meanwhile, our platform was growing. We were invited to speak at events, featured on podcasts, and highlighted in magazines and newspapers. It would've been easy to sit back and enjoy the spotlight, to focus on the growth of our influence. And, to be honest, we had to fight back against the natural tendency to protect our reputation rather than stand for truth (more on this in a minute).

But something inside us wouldn't let that happen. There was a fire burning deep down that we couldn't ignore. Sure, we could have avoided the collision with darkness—but doing so would mean forfeiting the impact we were called to make.

Oswald Chambers once said, "*The main characteristic which is the proof of the indwelling Spirit is an amazing tenderness in personal dealing and a blazing truthfulness with regard to God's Word.*"[15]

Here's a truth you need to remember: while God loves all people, He does not love all ideas.

As believers, we are called to treat every individual with kindness and compassion. But what about the bad ideas— the ones we know are harmful to people? What are we supposed to do with those?

We're not going to tell you what to do. The Bible does that for us:

"*We demolish arguments and every lofty opinion raised against the knowledge of God.*" (2 Corinthians 10:5).

The Greek word for "demolish" in this verse means to "destroy as with a wrecking ball."[16] Opinions and ideas that harm human beings should not be allowed free reign in culture without a standard of truth raised against them. Why? Because the knowledge of the truth is the only thing that sets people free.

"And you will know the truth, and the truth will set you free." (John 8:32).

If someone is sick, they need a doctor. If they are ignorant, they need a teacher. But if they are captive, they need a warrior! Today, people are being held captive by bad ideas that are keeping them enslaved in sinful lifestyles that harm them. It's time for believers to arise who love people enough to help set them free.

We chose to speak the truth about these hot-button issues, and it didn't take long for the backlash to hit. Almost overnight, we were labeled bigots, haters, and every kind of "-phobic" you can think of. This was back in 2010—long before *"cancel culture"* became a popular hashtag.

The harshest accusations leveled against us targeted our views on life and marriage. As we shared in chapter three, we were unapologetically pro-life and even started a ministry to support moms in need, which led to us being branded as "anti-women." Additionally, our commitment to standing for God's definition of marriage brought an onslaught of hateful labels—more than we ever could have imagined.

Of course, none of those accusations were true. They were just labels strategically used to silence us and discredit our message. So, by the time we signed Letters of Intent with HGTV, that false narrative was already circulating online. When their attorneys came across it, they quickly raised some concerns.

I (Jason) remember receiving a phone call from the production company explaining that the attorneys had questions about this online narrative. At that moment, I felt fear—a heavy fear—because I realized our platform, the opportunity to reach millions of homes, was now at risk.

HGTV was talking about putting us in millions of homes—a massive platform we were eager to use to share the hope of Jesus. But now, that platform was under threat. It was as if a voice in my head whispered, *"Hold on. If you don't handle this carefully, you could lose the very thing you and your brother have been working so hard for."*

Panic started to creep in, but in the middle of that emotional whirlwind, I fired off a quick prayer—a snap whisper to heaven asking God to bail me out and give me the right words. And wouldn't you know it, He answered. For the next five minutes, I said things I didn't even know I had in me. Honestly, I surprised myself at how good it was! Ha Ha.

Essentially, I said, *"Listen, we're not anti-anything, no matter what those labels might suggest. We're pro-Jesus, which means we're pro-Bible. We believe that God's blessings are found within His boundaries. If we remove the boundaries, blessings are replaced with burdens. So, if we truly care about people, we can't just talk about living a blessed life—we also need to talk about the boundaries we need to stay inside of to get those blessings."*

We set boundaries for our children, don't we? Not because we hate them but because we love them and want them to thrive. We hold firm even when they push back or insist we're being unfair. Why? Because we know that without learning to honor boundaries, the blessings in their lives will eventually be replaced by burdens.

I still remember her response on the call. She said, *"Oh, that's good. Most of us at the production company, everyone I know at HGTV, and even your agents—the same ones who represent the Kardashians in Beverly Hills—believe like you do, but none of us are willing to talk about it."*

Let that sink in for a moment. These people—many of them outside the "Christian bubble"—share our beliefs, yet they're too afraid to say so publicly. Why? Because they don't want to be vilified online the way we were.

This is exactly how evil operates. It erects a stronghold and then demonizes anyone brave enough to speak against it. It's a tactic designed to silence the truth and keep people in fear.

I hung up the phone and wiped the sweat off my forehead for dodging that bullet.

Or so I thought.

Two weeks passed—no phone calls, emails, or texts from HGTV, our agents, or the production company. I thought we were getting dumped. And I'd never been dumped before, so I had to turn to David for advice! (*That's so lame and not true -David*)

I remember calling David, saying, "*I don't think the attorneys liked my response. I think we're going to lose our show.*"

He echoed my sentiment, "*Yeah, I feel the same way.*"

So, we got together in our office, knelt down, and prayed. Our prayer sounded something like this, "*God, please save our show. Do you have any idea what we're going to do with this show? We're going to use it to tell people about you!*"

It sounded more like a negotiation than a prayer.

As we wrapped the prayer, I stood up and said, "*Let's write an email to HGTV and try to save our show.*"

David liked the idea, so he quickly wrote a draft and sent it to me for approval. Here's what it said:

"*HGTV, these are our beliefs, and we're never going to back off them…*"

Sounds pretty good, right? Well, we're not done yet.

"*…However, when we represent your network in public, we'll be quiet about them.*"

Now, don't judge me—he wrote it! Ha ha. He wrote it, and I approved it. Here's the scariest part: we both felt a sense of peace about it. But it was a false peace because, at that moment, we were operating out of a fear of man rather than a fear of God.

As a result, we started focusing on the platform we didn't want to lose rather than the person who put it there in the first place. And anytime you focus on what God has given you—the very thing he wants you to have—and you cling to it tightly, it becomes your idol.

The things you refuse to let go of are the very things that hold you captive.

That's where we found ourselves. We started operating strategically in the mind rather than spiritually in the heart. We were working *for* God no longer *with* God because we were fueled by fear rather than faith. All because we stopped focusing on God and started focusing on what we wanted from Him.

Have you ever been there?

We learned that when God gives you something, He wants you to hold it loosely, with open hands, and trust Him. But we didn't see that. We were deaf, blind, and dumb and didn't even know it. Our focus was off.

Well, we didn't send the email to HGTV right away. Instead, we decided to run it by a pastor friend we thought would agree. We knew better than to send it to our dad—we knew what he would say, and we weren't feeling that spiritual. So, we sent it to this pastor, hoping for some validation.

Within three minutes, he sent a reply that hit us like a ton of bricks. He said, "*How dare you boys write an email like this? This isn't who you are. How do you know that God isn't raising you up for such a time as this? He's not raising you up to have a reality show; He's raising you up to tear down a stronghold that's keeping Christians silent on things that matter. You don't need to send that email. You boys need to repent!*"

How about those apples? That response didn't feel very Christ-like, but it was exactly what we needed to hear. At that moment, we could imagine how Peter must have felt when he boldly promised Jesus that he would never deny Him, only to deny Him three times that very night. And when the rooster crowed, Peter was cut to the heart.

That email hit us the same way—it cut us to the heart. Conviction washed over us as we realized we had been operating out of a fear of man rather than a fear of God. And we knew what we had to do. Right then and there, we dropped to our knees and repented for being cowards when God was calling us to be courageous.

From that momentary lapse of faith, we learned a powerful truth: boldness, apart from brokenness, makes a bully.[17] God needed to break us of our fear of man, stripping away anything that kept us from fully trusting Him. He was preparing us for a time when we would need to stand boldly for Him—a time we couldn't yet see coming.

Ultimately, we discovered that the secret to courage is first recognizing your inner coward and then allowing the Holy Spirit to unleash your inner lion. Our *lion moment* was on the horizon, but first, we had to face our *coward moment*— because it prepared us for what was to come.

Thankfully, God forgave us and set us back on course. From that point forward, we were ready for whatever came our way—whether the show happened or not. Either way, our hearts were settled: we would trust God no matter what.

After nearly three weeks of silence, the executive producer called a few days later and said, "*Guys, are we doing this or what? Let's get filming.*"

They acknowledged the negative narrative circulating online but assured us they knew it wasn't true and were ready to move forward. HGTV's top executives were on board and eager to get started.

To say we were surprised by their enthusiasm would be an understatement. It was amazing to see that they could see past the lies, rise above the noise, and make a fair, objective decision to work with us.

After wrapping up the pilot for *Fixer Upper*, HGTV brought the showrunners from Waco to oversee our show. Before we knew it, the Spring of 2014 had arrived, and we were already five weeks into a 10-week filming schedule. Commercials for the show were airing, everything was on track, and the momentum felt unstoppable.

Then, one evening around 9:00 PM, just after finishing our fifth week of filming, David's phone rang. It was the general manager, and her voice was full of excitement.

"Guys, this is great!" she said. *"All the advertisers are coming in, and they're loving the direction of your show. But there's a small issue—an activist group out of California isn't so happy. They're upset we gave you a show and are pointing to the online narrative about you."*

"But don't worry," she added. *"We told them it's a false narrative. We're standing by you because we believe you will be stars on this network."*

It felt good to hear that. We went to bed that night, relishing the fact that a company as large as HGTV would stand up for us like that.

HERE COMES THE BOOM

The following day, we woke up to our phones buzzing with texts from friends all over the country. They asked what was happening with our show and if we'd seen HGTV's Facebook page. We had no idea what they were talking about.

So, we pulled up the page, and there it was—one single sentence at the top: *"We are reviewing the Benham Brothers' show."* Beneath it were hundreds of comments—vile, hateful remarks about us, our wives, and even our kids. It was shocking and disgusting.

Apparently, the activist group out of California wasn't satisfied with HGTV's support. So they tapped one of their media allies to write a fresh hit piece about the "bigoted Benhams" and blasted it across the internet. The article was published and went viral within hours, shaming HGTV for daring to give us a platform.

By this point, we were considered public figures, and the rules are different for them. You can lie, smear, and spread falsehoods about them without facing legal repercussions—something you can't do to private citizens. Sadly, we see this happening all the time in America today, with the mainstream media twisting narratives and spreading outright lies about people. That's exactly what they did to us, painting us as fools.

The attacks were relentless, part of a calculated smear campaign. One of the most outrageous claims was that we had stood in front of a mosque shouting, *"God hates Muslims."* The truth? God loves Muslims, and we've never even set foot in a mosque our entire lives. It was a blatant, malicious lie—fabricated to discredit us and fuel the outrage.

We had no idea how to respond or what to do next. The only thing we knew for sure was that we had a 9:00 AM call time that morning at one of the houses we were remodeling. So, we showed up to the set as planned. While we were getting ready to shoot, my phone buzzed with a text from HGTV's general manager: *"Can you guys hop on a quick call with me and a couple of our executives this morning?"*

"Sure," we replied. We found a quiet spot, put the phone on speaker, and dialed in. The call was brief and straight to the point. *"Guys, we're canceling the show,"* she said.

After I (Jason) got David out of the fetal position and pried his thumb from his mouth, we both took a deep breath. Our first response? *"Thank you. Thank you for believing in us."* Then we added, "Romans 8:28 says, *'All things work together for good.'"*

"I wasn't prepared to be speechless on this call," she responded. *"That's very gracious of you both."*

The other two executives didn't say a word. One of them was crying.

Our hearts went out to them. We knew this wasn't the decision they wanted to make, but the rest of their executive team felt overwhelmed, as if the weight of the world were crashing down on them. Because of this article, they feared the repercussions of having two guys on their network who openly supported Biblical values.

After the call ended, we sat there in stunned silence. Just like that, the dream we'd been so excited about was over. But deep down, we knew this wasn't the end of the story—God was still writing it.

Later that day, we emailed the executive team. "*We know you believed in us,*" we said. "*But you got bullied into this. There's a Goliath in culture that demands silence from Christians, and we have no intention of backing down.*"

We had no idea what was coming next, but one thing was certain—we'd already had our "cowardly" moment. Now, it was time to step up and be courageous, no matter what lay ahead.

Word of our firing spread like wildfire, and before we knew it, our phones were flooded with requests from news outlets eager to tell our story. Over the next several months, we conducted close to 200 one-on-one interviews with major networks, including *CNN*, *FOX News*, *Good Morning America*, and *Nightline*.

We were even featured on HBO with Bill Maher, who called us the "*nitwit twin brothers who believe in the same dumb book that millions of Americans believe.*" At that moment, Christ's words in Luke 21, warning believers about certain persecution, became very real for us. We experienced a level of persecution for our faith that we had never faced before.

The most shocking part, however, was that these groups weren't satisfied with us simply losing our show—they wanted to destroy us completely. They targeted our businesses and even went after our banks. Damaging our reputation wasn't enough for them; they were determined to ruin us financially.

Here's the cool part: as much damage as they managed to inflict on our active business income, there was one thing they couldn't touch and didn't even know about—our passive investment income.

Suckers :)

They couldn't lay a finger on our real estate. Financially, we were bulletproof. And in today's cancel culture, that felt pretty incredible.

But do you know what felt even better and still feels amazing to this day? We're spiritually bulletproof—and so are you!

"For greater is He who is in us than he who is in the world" (1 John 4:4).

We have *nothing* to fear! Fear is one of Satan's favorite tools—it's how he keeps us paralyzed and silent. We know this because we've felt its grip firsthand. But here's what we discovered: your greatest blessing is often found on the other side of your greatest fear.

So don't back down. Don't let fear dictate your steps. Fix your focus on God—not on the thing you're afraid of losing—and watch what He does.

God wants to move in your life *right now.* He wants to move in this nation. Billy Graham once said he believed the next great move of God would happen among believers in the workplace. That's our prayer, our belief, and the heartbeat behind this book.

In the next chapter, we'll share the practical steps we took to become financially bulletproof. And while financial security is valuable, the *real* goal isn't about the income you make—it's about the *impact* you leave behind.

This is not a time for believers to shrink back in fear. It's a time to surge forward by faith.

So, what about you? The world may try to silence you, intimidate you, or even take what you have—but they can't touch what matters most. If you are anchored in Christ, you are spiritually bulletproof. And when you learn to build streams of passive income, you can become financially bulletproof as well.

This is not a time to cower, compromise, or back down. It's a time to stand firm, to rise up in faith, and to let the light of Jesus shine through you, whatever the cost.

CHAPTER EIGHT

SIX STEPS TO FINANCIAL FREEDOM

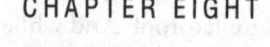

*"Being rich is having money.
Being wealthy is having time."*

– Margaret Bannano

When financial success came our way, the greatest blessing wasn't just the ability to give our money away—it was the time it bought us to give *ourselves* away.

I (David) once heard someone say, *"There are only two problems in the world: money problems and people problems. If you solve the money problem, you can focus on people for the rest of your life."*

I'm not sure whether or not that's entirely true, but I love the heart behind it. Solving the money problem frees us to invest our time, energy, and lives into the people God places around us. And isn't that what it's all about?

Currently, I am sitting in a hotel room on a Saturday morning without a thought in the world of how I'm going to make money today. The residual income I receive each month buys me time *so I can give my time to you* by writing this book. That's not a pat on my back. It's simply an acknowledgment of where you can be if you apply the principles we've taught you in this book and follow the steps we'll teach you in this chapter.

We will show you the exact steps we took to achieve financial freedom, providing a financial structure that will allow you to buy your time back. This type of freedom will set you free and position you for greater impact. As we shared in the last chapter, it will make you financially bulletproof.

Before we jump in, there's something vitally important you need to settle first: *your why.* Before we even started the journey of turning our active income into passive income—following the principles of Proverbs 27, which we discussed in chapter six—we had to get crystal clear on *why* we were doing it. We had to ask ourselves, *"If God chooses to bless these efforts, what will we do with the time and freedom that follow?"*

Knowing your *why* isn't just helpful—it's essential.

At first, our *why* was pretty straightforward—we just wanted to provide for our families. It wasn't anything grand or noble, like building an orphanage or funding a major ministry, but it was an honest and legitimate reason to get started.

However, we quickly realized that if we wanted to build something truly significant, our purpose needed to expand. So, we took a step back. We spent time thinking, praying, and reflecting—digging through our experiences, influences, and everything God had shown us along the way. We wanted our *why* to anchor us as we moved forward because financial freedom can lose its meaning without a clear purpose.

We kept coming back to how our parents always told us we had the "gift of gab," and they knew God would use it one day to help others. As students, we used it to disrupt classes with well-timed jokes. As athletes, we used it to argue with umpires about bad calls. But as adults, we wanted to use it to help others grow close to God.

When we launched our first business in 2003, before financial success ever came our way, we took time to think deeply about what we wanted to accomplish if we reached our goals. After much prayer and reflection, we crafted a simple statement that has guided us ever since. Today, we teach it in our coaching programs and call it our *SO THAT* statement. Here's what we wrote:

- We want to be financially free *SO THAT* we can minister to people through speaking and writing.

We loved the idea of not having to trade our time for money but for ideas. The question that helped us understand this was: "*What would we do if money wasn't an issue?*" That's a great question for you as well.

If you didn't have to think about money, how would you spend your time to make a difference in the lives of others?

Influencing others through speaking and writing was our answer to that question.

If God chooses to bless your efforts and you become financially free, what will you do with your newfound time? What is your *so that* statement?

Take some time to think about it now. The rest of this chapter is devoted to giving you the practical plan that will help you get there.

Here's what we're going to cover:

- Turning Your Grip into a Drip: a mindset for how to think about money.

- Three-Budget Plan: developing financial targets that serve as boundaries to stay within and goals to achieve.

- Six-Step "Grip to Drip" Process: the money map we used to achieve freedom from financial stress.

GRIP TO DRIP

As we discussed in Chapter Four, while Bon Jovi may sing about giving love a bad name, when it comes to money, the secret to financial freedom is to give cash a *last* name.

Your cash needs to become *cash flow*.

We first heard this concept when we read Robert Kiyosaki's book *Rich Dad, Poor Dad* while in pro baseball. He taught that you could turn the cash in your bank account into a passive income stream by investing that money into income-producing assets. By doing so, you turn your cash into cash flow. Or, as we've come to say, you turn your *grip* (money in the bank—your bucket) into a *drip* (money from investments—your river).

Your grip is your active income—the money you make from your job or business. What we're suggesting is that you set aside some of that active income—your grip—and use it to purchase cash-producing assets. That's your drip— things you own that produce money without your direct management or effort—passive income. If you stay at it long enough, that drip becomes a sizable stream and maybe even a massive river.

Your income stream could include shares in mutual funds, index funds, or other interest-producing financial products. You could also invest in income-producing real estate and small businesses, as we did.

There are several other good sources of drip income, but we chose long-term rental real estate because it has historically proven to be one of the most powerful engines for creating a steady stream of constantly replenishing "drip" income.

The point isn't what form your stream takes—it's that you start creating it. To do that, we need to start by defining your target.

THREE BUDGETS

Once you grasp the concept of turning your cash into *cash flow*, the next step is to set clear financial goals. Aiming for one big, overwhelming number felt discouraging and out of reach for us. So, we broke it down into three smaller, manageable targets. We later called it our Three-Budget Plan because it turned out to be one of the best things we've done to help us stay on the path to financial freedom.

We created the following three budgets:

- A Livable Budget—what we'd *need.*

- A Comfortable Budget—what we'd *like.*

- An Incredible Budget—what we'd *love.*

We assigned a dollar value to each of these to quantify our goals. Many people fail to quantify how much is enough, so they pursue money endlessly until the day they die. Like John D. Rockefeller, when asked how much it would take to make a man happy, he replied, *"Just one more dollar."*[18]

That's not the path of a kingdom wealth builder. We must quantify how much is enough.

Our *livable* budget was the monthly income we could literally survive on *if we had to.* We're talking bare-bones-type stuff. On this budget, you'd have to get rid of your lawn service crew and pool cleaning, and whatever else is not 100 percent necessary.

When we first started, our livable budget was around $2,500 a month. This was back in 2003 when rent was cheap, and eggs didn't cost a thousand bucks, so those numbers are nearly impossible nowadays. But the key is to keep your livable number as lean as humanly possible.

Our *comfortable* budget was the amount of monthly income we could comfortably live on. This budget allowed us to live our lives without worrying about pinching pennies. We could send our kids to good schools, get our lawn serviced, and afford a few containers of mocha-chocolate-chip ice cream to eat when we watched the Cowboys play.

Our *incredible* budget was the monthly income we dreamed of having—an amount that would allow us to go on overseas family trips, afford college without loans, leave an inheritance for our kids, and give abundantly to nonprofit efforts that are doing great things in the world.

As a point of reference, here's an example of what the three budget numbers could look like:

- Livable - $5,000 a month

- Comfortable $12,500 a month

- Incredible - $25,000 a month

The dollar amounts will vary depending on your goals. We've coached people with budgets well below these numbers and others with budgets that dwarfed them.

Having our budget numbers in place prevented us from developing "Rockefeller syndrome." It gave us goals to aim for and boundaries to adhere to, making our financial decisions much easier and motivating us to achieve our goals.

With those numbers firmly ingrained in our heads, we devised a specific plan for covering each one—first, with our active income from our work and then, with our passive income from our investments. Our process involved six steps.

SIX-STEP "GRIP TO DRIP" PROCESS

We will share here the map we followed to turn the *riches* we earned from our work into *wealth* gained through investments. If you follow these steps methodically and put in the required effort, you'll be well on your way to achieving the financial goals you've set for yourself.

Steps 1-3 focus on your *active* income from the work you do.

Steps 4-6 focus on using your active income to build your *passive* investment income.

All six steps utilize the three budget numbers derived earlier.

Step One: *Cover your livable budget with active income.*

This is simply about finding a job with enough income to cover your basic needs. Most of you reading this book are already well past this stage, so we won't dwell on it. However, it's essential to teach your kids this critical first step!

The Bible is clear: "*The one who is unwilling to work shall not eat*" (2 Thessalonians 3:10).

Step Two: *Cover your comfortable budget with active income.*

This is the stage where you climb the ladder in your job or business by increasing the value you bring to your boss, team, or customers. As believers, our role in the workplace is to work with excellence—doing such a great job that we not only glorify God but also become more valuable to those we serve. And money follows value.

After completing Step Two, it might seem logical to assume that Step Three involves covering your incredible budget with active income. But that would be incorrect.

Step Three: *Set aside the surplus.*

This step separates those who achieve financial freedom from those who don't. It's tough because you're making money *above* your comfortable budget, and that money is sitting there screaming at you, "Spend me!" But hear us on this—DO NOT TAKE IT FOR YOURSELF! That time will come later on.

This is where a little delayed gratification can go a long way. According to studies, the number one predictor of success isn't education or the wealth of your parents or even natural intelligence and talent—it's whether or not you can delay gratification.[19]

If you can't say "no" to your natural impulse to take the money, your hopes of becoming financially free will be short-lived. But if you have the discipline to leave that money alone, you can use it for crucial Step Four.

These next three steps are where you use your active income to build your passive income.

Step Four: *Cover your livable budget with passive income from investments.*

Remember, in stage one, you covered your livable budget with *active* income from your work. Now, your goal is to cover it with *passive* income from your investments.

Step Four is where you invest the surplus above your comfortable budget into income-producing assets.

As we said earlier, we started by investing primarily in real estate. We started slowly, but the next thing we knew, we owned a handful of rental properties. Soon, passive income from these investments completely covered our livable budget.

Hear this: When your passive income exceeds your bare-bones living expenses, you are *financially free*! You can now live without ever having to work for money again if you don't want to.

Let that sink in.

Imagine the feeling of going to work because you WANT to and not because you HAVE to.

But we're not done yet; there are two more steps to go.

Step Five: *Cover your comfortable budget with passive income from investments.*

Let's be clear—at this stage, we were still living well below our means despite the success of our business. In addition, income from newly formed passive streams started flowing in. But instead of spending it or increasing our salaries, we added every extra dollar to our surplus of active income and kept reinvesting it. This decision exponentially supercharged the pace of our "Grip to Drip" plan.

Before we knew it, we had enough passive income to cover our comfortable budget number. At this point, we could take ourselves off the company payroll if we wanted to, and nothing about our way of life would change. That was an amazing feeling.

This is the stage where you move from being financially free to *independently wealthy*. You can live a comfortable lifestyle for the rest of your life, independent of any job or day-to-day effort.

From that point forward, we began aggressively investing in passive income vehicles with every drop of our surplus active income *and* all the extra passive income earnings.

Fortunately, the more we ran our business and worked according to Biblical principles, the more active income we generated. So, we invested that additional money in more investments while keeping our salaries at the same moderate level.

But there's one more step, which happens to be the best of all.

Step Six: *Cover your incredible budget with passive income from your investments.*

Getting to Step Six is where you can give away more money than you ever imagined and live a life you never dreamed of. Even better, it's a place so incredible that you'll want nothing more than to help others experience the same.

From then on, you have the freedom to do only what you *want*. Whether you're an employee or a business owner, this is where the game changes. If you're working a job, you're no longer tied to it out of necessity—you're there because you choose to be. You can focus on roles and projects that bring you joy, align with your purpose, and contribute to your vision and mission.

This is the beauty of financial independence—it's not about stepping away from work altogether; it's about stepping into work that matters most to you.

Reaching Stage Six isn't a sprint—it's a marathon. So be patient. This six-step plan isn't some *"Get Rich Quick"* scheme. God's way has always been more like *"Get Rich Slowly."*

"...whoever gathers money little by little makes it grow" (Proverbs 13:11).

The key is consistency. Keep applying the principles you've learned, trust God to guide and provide, and remember—you don't have to reach the finish line today. Just take the next step forward.

Here is the plan in picture format:

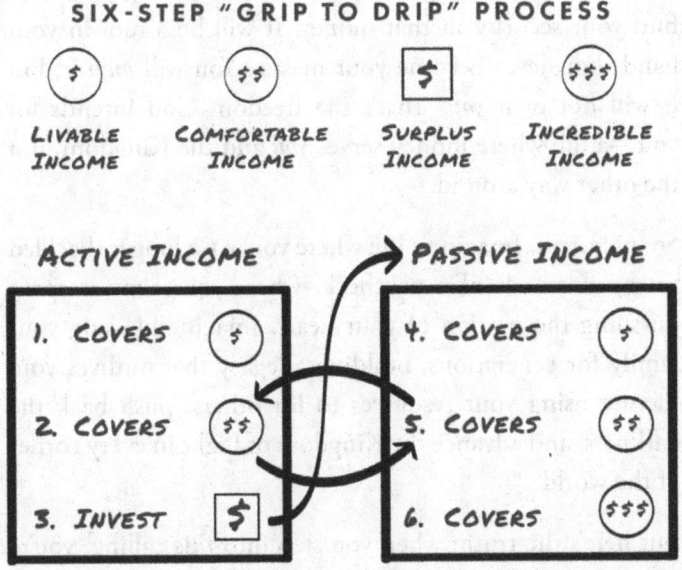

SIX-STEP "GRIP TO DRIP" PROCESS

$	$$	$	$$$
LIVABLE INCOME	COMFORTABLE INCOME	SURPLUS INCOME	INCREDIBLE INCOME

ACTIVE INCOME → PASSIVE INCOME

1. COVERS $
2. COVERS $$
3. INVEST $

4. COVERS $
5. COVERS $$
6. COVERS $$$

No matter where you are in your financial journey, the concepts we've shared will help you achieve a life you never dreamed possible—one that can impact the lives of others for generations to come.

It doesn't take rocket science. You don't have to be a brain surgeon. You just need a little discipline, a lot of determination, and a willingness to stick to the plan. And you, too, can turn your grip into a drip—a steady stream of money that replenishes itself without your direct involvement ...every day and night for the rest of your life.

And best of all, when you build wealth God's way, you won't find your security in that money. It will be a tool in your hands but never become your master. You will *own* it, but it will not own *you*. That's the freedom God intends for you—a life where money serves *you* and the Kingdom, not the other way around.

So, picture it. Imagine a life where you're no longer shackled to the demands of a paycheck, where your time is spent pursuing the passion of your heart. Imagine blessing your family for generations, building a legacy that outlives you. Picture using your resources to lift others, push back the darkness, and advance the Kingdom of Light in every corner of the world.

But here's the truth: when you step into this calling, you're stepping straight into the collision between the Kingdom of Light and the Kingdom of Darkness. The enemy won't sit back quietly—he'll resist you, he'll attack you, and he'll try to keep you sidelined. But don't shrink back. Embrace the collision! You're on the winning side. You are called to this fight, and you are equipped to overcome it.

Now, stop imagining it—and go *build* it. Because that's who you are: a spiritual warrior created by God to cultivate, to multiply, and to steward generational wealth. You're not just here to make a living—you're here to make a difference. So rise up, take hold of what God has placed in your hands, and run boldly into the fight.

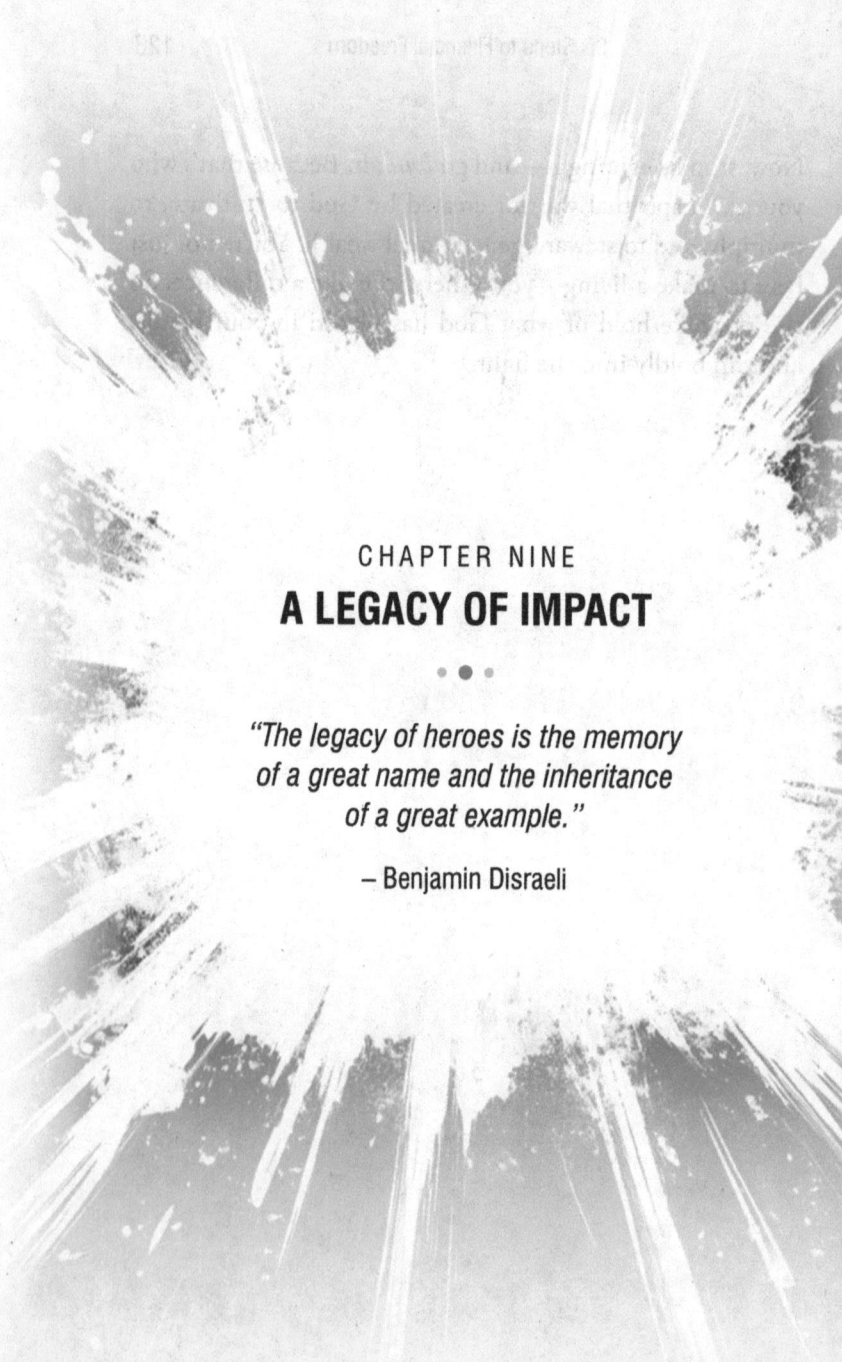

CHAPTER NINE

A LEGACY OF IMPACT

• ● •

*"The legacy of heroes is the memory
of a great name and the inheritance
of a great example."*

– Benjamin Disraeli

Before we close this book, we want to tell you about a few historical figures whose lives bring to life the principles we've shared in these pages. They demonstrate how to use wealth to create a lasting impact and stand firm when faced with the inevitable collision that comes with living boldly.

When the fires of persecution came our way, we drew strength from the example of these two men from the 1800s who risked their lives and fortunes to push back the darkness of their time. It felt good to know that our story was nothing new. Their boldness encouraged us to stand strong, whatever the cost.

We first learned about these brothers early in our business careers, back in our twenties, when an unexpected visitor showed up at our office. He looked disheveled, like he hadn't showered in a few days, and asked one of our assistants if he could speak with us. He claimed to have an urgent message for us—a direct word from God.

Naturally, our assistant hesitated. She figured this guy was a little off his rocker. But after some thought, she asked if we'd be willing to hear him out.

We had the same reservations she had, but something nudged us about taking the meeting. After all, what if God did have something to say through this man? John the Baptist wasn't exactly polished either, right? So, we decided to give him a few minutes of our time.

When we walked into the conference room, the man was practically glowing with excitement—not because he was meeting with us, but because he couldn't wait to share what he had to say. Clutching a wrinkled piece of paper covered in scribbled notes, he explained that God had woken him up in the middle of the night with a message for us. He wrote it down to make sure he didn't forget.

"Have you heard of the Tappan brothers?" he asked, barely able to contain his enthusiasm.

"No," we replied.

"You have to read everything you can about these two brothers," he said, his voice brimming with urgency. "They were wealthy business owners in the 1800s who leveraged their lives and fortunes to push back the darkness of their day. Few people know their names, but if you look at some of the most significant moves of God in America's history— the abolition of slavery, women's rights, the Second Great Awakening—the Tappans were working behind the scenes, using their platform and their resources to help make it all happen."

He couldn't sit still. Pacing the room, he explained how God had given him a mandate to tell us about these brothers. He passionately declared that God was raising up modern-day wealthy warriors to stand in the gap and push back the darkness of our time. He believed we were meant to step into that calling.

We ended up talking with him for over an hour. His passion inspired us deeply, and his words lit a fire in our hearts. He encouraged us to keep building our business, not just for success, but so we could increase our wealth and use it for Kingdom impact, just like the Tappan brothers had done.

When the meeting ended, we did exactly what he suggested—we researched everything we could about these brothers. What we found was nothing short of incredible. Their story challenged and motivated us in ways we never expected, shaping how we thought about our role in the workplace.

The Tappan brothers weren't just successful businessmen—they were trailblazers who leveraged their wealth to make a Kingdom impact that echoes through history. To this day, their lives challenge us to see money not as a means of personal comfort but as a powerful tool for transformation. They remind us that when used with courage and conviction, wealth can push back the darkness and leave an enduring legacy.

The Tappans built their fortune in the silk-importing business during the early 1800s in New York. They were sharp, innovative entrepreneurs who ran their businesses with integrity and fairness. They paid fair wages, refused to operate on Sundays (like Chic-Fil-A and Hobby Lobby), and held themselves to the highest ethical standards. But what truly set them apart was their conviction that wealth wasn't meant for self-indulgence—it was meant for impact. To them, money wasn't just a resource; it was a responsibility.

The Tappans weren't just committed to treating people fairly—they were sharp entrepreneurs who knew how to navigate the twists and turns of global trade. They built reliable supply chains, forged strong partnerships overseas, and ensured their products met the highest standards of quality. Their innovative business practices, paired with solid financial management, helped them grow their wealth significantly. And here's the best part—that success gave them the freedom to invest deeply in causes that mattered. They proved that you don't have to choose between running a profitable business and making a meaningful difference. You can do both and do them well.

Rooted in their Christian faith and influenced by Charles Finney's preaching during the Second Great Awakening, the Tappans believed they were called to care for the oppressed, uplift the vulnerable, and advance Godly causes. Their financial success gave them the freedom to focus on a higher purpose: building a society rooted in justice, compassion, and righteousness. And they didn't wait for someone else to step up. They rolled up their sleeves and invested their time and resources to turn their convictions into action.

The Tappans played a pivotal role in the *Benevolent Empire,* a network of Christian organizations tackling the pressing social issues of their day. Poverty, illiteracy, slavery, and alcohol addiction were rampant in 19th-century America, but the Tappans and their allies saw these challenges as opportunities to destroy strongholds and bring flourishing.

Through the Benevolent Empire, the Tappans funded and led initiatives aimed at transforming society. They supported the American Bible Society, distributing God's Word across the nation, believing it had the power to change lives. They backed the American Tract Society, producing and spreading Christian literature to instill moral values. They were also active in the temperance movement, promoting sobriety to strengthen families and communities.

Their efforts weren't about band-aid solutions; they were about cultural transformation. The Tappans and their allies weren't satisfied with treating symptoms—they were committed to addressing the root causes of societal issues. Their vision was bold: to bring about America's moral and spiritual renewal, no matter the cost.

One of their greatest legacies is their leadership in the abolitionist movement. The Tappans were among the first and most fervent voices calling for the end of slavery, dedicating their wealth and influence to dismantle this horrific institution. In 1833, they co-founded the American Anti-Slavery Society, a driving force in the abolitionist movement.

Arthur Tappan served as the society's first president, while both brothers provided significant financial support to sustain its mission. They funded abolitionist newspapers, like *The Liberator*, to spread the anti-slavery message. They sponsored public lectures, rallies, and petitions to awaken the conscience of the nation. And they didn't stop there. The Tappans used their wealth to protect and assist those escaping slavery, funding legal defenses for fugitive slaves and supporting the Underground Railroad.

Their commitment to education was just as bold. The Tappans championed equal access to learning, funding Oberlin College—a groundbreaking institution that welcomed both Black students and women at a time when such inclusivity was unheard of. Their investment in education wasn't just financial; it was a courageous stand for a future where every human being had the right to thrive. It was a vision rooted in Christian faith and fueled by a relentless belief in God's view of justice.

Of course, their boldness came at a cost. The Tappans faced relentless opposition. Pro-slavery advocates boycotted their businesses, causing financial losses. Mobs attacked their home and offices, destroying property and threatening their lives. Their reputations were constantly under fire, yet they stood firm. Their unwavering conviction reminds us that making an impact involves a collision—but the rewards of standing for what is right far outweigh the risks.

Their resilience is a powerful reminder that making an impact often requires stepping out of our comfort zones. It's not always easy to do the right thing, especially when it costs us something. But the Tappans' story shows us that courage and conviction can overcome even the fiercest opposition.

The Tappan brothers' lives are a testament to the power of aligning wealth with purpose. Their story challenges us to rethink how we use our resources. Imagine the impact we could have if we used our income the way they did—not just to make a living but to make a difference. They prove that a life of purpose and generosity can reshape the world, even in the face of opposition.

So, what will you do with what you've been given? Like the Tappan brothers, you have the power to leave a legacy that matters. Let their story inspire you—as it inspired us—to dream big, act boldly, and invest your resources in something that will outlast you. Because when you do, you're not just spending money—you're shaping history.

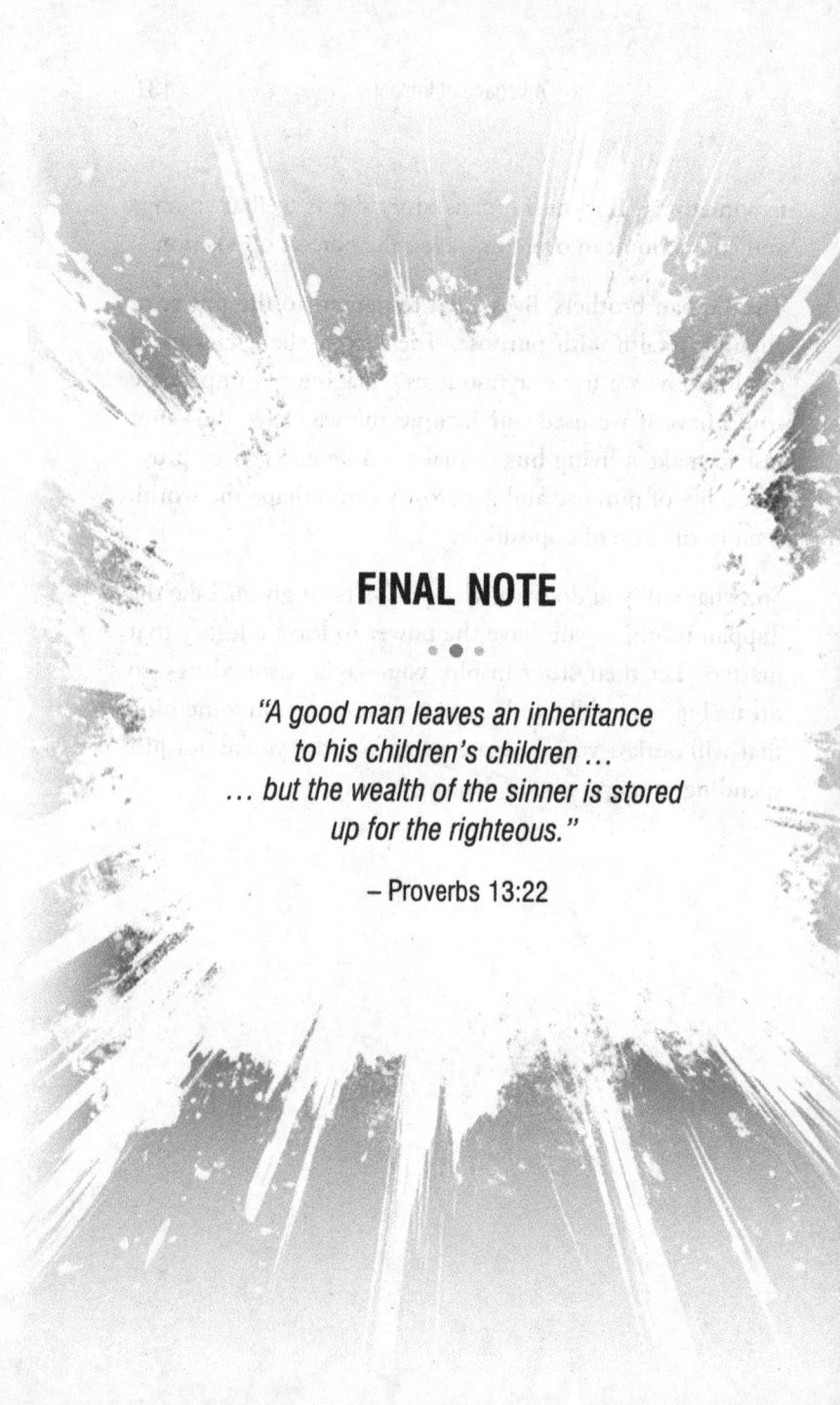

FINAL NOTE

• • •

*"A good man leaves an inheritance
to his children's children …
… but the wealth of the sinner is stored
up for the righteous."*

– Proverbs 13:22

Every month, we try to read through the book of Proverbs. As we mentioned earlier, it was written by King Solomon— the wisest and arguably the wealthiest man in history. We've been doing this for a few decades now, which means we've each read Proverbs a few hundred times (give or take—we're investors, not mathematicians!).

We've read plenty of books on wealth over the years, but we can say with absolute confidence that Proverbs is by far the best book on growing wealth and maximizing impact. If you're not already reading this book on a consistent basis, add it to your VIP list of content you consume. You won't be disappointed.

A recurring theme in Proverbs is the stark contrast between the prosperity of the righteous and the downfall of the wicked. Of course, we don't always see it play out that way in this life—but that's a conversation for another time.

So, what sets the two apart? Pastor Timothy Keller offered some valuable insight:

"The righteous in the book of Proverbs are by definition those who are willing to disadvantage themselves for the community while the wicked are those who put their own economic, social, and personal needs ahead of the needs of the community."[20]

Proverbs 11:10 is the classic example of the contrast between the two:

"When the righteous prosper, the city rejoices; when the wicked perish, there are shouts of joy."

Why does a city rejoice when a righteous person prospers? Because their prosperity doesn't just benefit them—it blesses the entire community. They use their resources to make an impact, improving the lives of those around them.

The wicked, however, are driven by selfishness and greed. They prioritize their own desires over the needs of others, leaving no positive legacy behind. No one mourns their absence when they're gone—in fact, their departure is often a reason to celebrate.

If you want your community, city, and nation to celebrate your financial success, prioritize living righteously! Righteousness means being in a "right relationship" with God. A key characteristic of righteous people is their commitment to using their resources to bless others and create a meaningful impact in their community.

What's the reward for living this way? Proverbs 13:22 tells us:

"...the wealth of the sinner (wicked) is laid up for the righteous." (emphasis added)

Back in chapter five, we introduced the first part of this verse when we talked about the three aspects of wealth. But we intentionally held off on sharing the second part until now. Why? Because we wanted to close this book with a powerful reminder:

God is in the "transfer" business.

Proverbs 13:22 assures us that, ultimately, the wealth of the wicked will be handed over to the righteous. This promise means we don't need to exhaust ourselves by chasing the latest financial trends. Our calling is to remain in right relationship with God, putting the needs of others before our own and using the resources He's entrusted to us to bless our communities—leaving the transfer in His hands.

We want to play a role in this wealth transfer, and there's nothing we'd love more than to see you among the righteous who receive it—using it to advance God's Kingdom and take a stand against darkness. This book is just one small step in that journey.

As we close, we pray that you've come to see wealth as far more than dollars and cents. It's about stewarding what God has entrusted to you—caring for your family, transforming your community, and pushing back the darkness in this world.

Throughout these chapters, we've unpacked biblical principles for wealth—principles that free us from the love of money while equipping us to use it as a tool for good. We've seen that God doesn't just want us to have riches for the sake of comfort; He wants us to build wealth that creates freedom—freedom to serve others and to impact the world for Christ.

We've discussed turning your active income into passive income and creating rivers instead of filling buckets. We've also shown you how to follow the *Proverbs 27* approach to living below your means, multiplying what you have, and positioning your family for generations of blessing. But remember this: all the financial wisdom in the world is useless if we lose sight of our *why*.

Why are we building wealth? Why are we aiming for financial freedom? It's not just to retire early or live an easy life—it's to have the time and resources to give ourselves away. Wealth done God's way positions us to step into the collision between the Kingdom of Light and the Kingdom of Darkness—and to *win*.

But let's be clear: this journey won't be without cost. The enemy will oppose you every step of the way. You will face resistance and be tempted to shrink back in fear or cling too tightly to what you've built. Don't let it happen. Remember, you are not alone in this fight. You are a spiritual warrior, equipped by God to stand firm, to multiply, and to make a difference in the world.

The legacy you build is not just for you—it's for your children and your children's children. It's for the broken, the lost, and the oppressed who need to see hope in action. Your wealth is not just income—it's an opportunity for greater impact.

So, as you step out to build, invest, and grow, be bold, embrace the collision, and let God use your life—and your wealth—to write a story that echoes into eternity. (cue the Gladiator theme song!)

JOIN US ON THE **JOURNEY**

If you enjoyed this book, it's just the beginning of a collection of resources available to help you become the Kingdom builder God designed you to be. Visit ExpertOwnership.com to learn more about our courses, coaching, and community.

As a gift to you for completing this book, please visit Blueprint4Impact.com and gain access to our four-part online course Blueprint For Impact, where we walk you through four phases of impact:

- Mission
- Money
- Margin
- Mindspace

This course is a battle-proven blueprint for thriving in business without gaining everything and missing the mark. Use coupon code IMPACT to get it for free.

Enjoy.

For business owners considering personal coaching options to help you save more time, make more money, and have a greater impact, contact us at Info@ExpertOwnership.com. You can also visit our website and take our free entrepreneurial assessment to see where you are in your business journey.

Visit ExpertOwnership.com for more information.

We'll see you on the other side!

David & Jason

APPENDIX

WEALTHY EXAMPLES

• • •

"Example is not the main thing in influencing others; it's the only thing."

– Albert Einstein

As we conclude this book, we would be remiss not to acknowledge a few key people who helped shape our understanding of wealth and demonstrated how to use it for lasting impact. While our parents were instrumental in modeling godly principles during our younger years, they weren't the only ones. In His providence, God brought several other men into our lives who played vital roles in preparing and shaping us for the future He had in store.

These men showed us firsthand that financial success paves the way for you to bless people greatly. Their example lodged deep in our hearts, and the generosity we saw in them became a burning passion of ours as we began to experience financial abundance.

Shortly after Dad lost his position in the church, the two of us boys were playing catch in the street when a family friend, Mr. Dave White, pulled up in his Mercedes Benz with Dad in the passenger seat. Dad got out with a shoebox in his hand, walked over to us, and lifted the lid. Inside were the nicest, most expensive dress shoes we'd ever seen. Mr. Dave, like a lot of other successful businessmen, was a "shoe guy," and he didn't want to buy himself a pair without getting our dad a new pair as well.

It may seem like a petty thing, but at the time, it spoke volumes to all of us that Mr. Dave cared enough to put the finest shoes money could buy on a pastor who was sidelined for standing true to his convictions. He did this for several years after that, and it became a tradition Dad always looked forward to. Dave's generosity etched in our hearts a passion to one day be in a position to do the same.

Richard Couron was another man who had a lasting impact on our lives. He and his family started coming to church when it was held in our house. We didn't know it then, but Richard was a serial entrepreneur who owned a leading tech company that was uber-successful. You'd never know it by the modest house he had or the van he drove. (Admittedly, we were a little jealous of the Zodiac shoes and Z. Cavaricci pants his sons, David and Ricky, wore. If you grew up in the '80s, you know wearing those brands meant you had *arrived*. Maybe that's why all the girls liked them more than us.) *(Actually, I think it was Jason's chili-bowl haircut that turned them away)*.

Richard was good to our family throughout his time in the church—a little gift here, a little check there. He was devastated when Dad got the ax from the pastorate, but he also saw God's hand leading Dad into full-time pro-life work. He wanted to ensure Dad could stay there without feeling the heavy financial pressure of raising a family, so he put him on his payroll.

Who does that?

Richard showed us the incredible impact a God-fearing, Gospel-centered believer can have in the workplace. He changed countless lives by excelling in his work and being generous with his earnings. We can't even begin to count the number of babies saved because of our dad's tireless efforts at abortion clinics across America. But behind the scenes stood an unsung hero—the godly wealth-builder whose faith and generosity helped make it all possible.

Here's the cool part: Richard kept Dad on his payroll until the day we were able to put him on ours. For more than 20 years now, Dad has been on our payroll—a legacy we wear as a badge of honor.

Both Mr. Dave and Richard are dead and gone now, but their legacies live on. While our dad showed us what faithfulness looked like as a pastor, these men showed us what faithfulness looked like in the workplace and how a generous spirit paves the way for impact in life.

As much as we wanted to be like our dad *spiritually*, we also wanted to be like those men *financially*. We didn't thirst for money, but we wanted the ability to bless people in big ways and support godly initiatives as they did. (*Maybe we wanted to be able to afford some Zodiacs and Z. Cavariccis, too.*)

Mr. Dave and Richard demonstrated the power of using your income to bless people, impact communities, and even change a culture.

But God didn't stop there. Just before we graduated from college, He brought another man into our lives, inspiring us in our business journey in ways we could never have imagined.

His name was David Drye. He was a wealthy businessman who inspired us so much that simply meeting him changed the trajectory of our lives. Mr. Drye was the first person we saw run his business as a ministry—not just with his profits but also with his process. This motivated us to operate in the same way when we started our company years later.

Mr. Drye, a friend of our father's, was a man of many talents. He ran a successful business, operated a Christian school, and hosted a Christian television show. He lived in Concord, North Carolina, conveniently located along our route from Dallas to Liberty University in Virginia. When Dad mentioned we'd be passing through, Mr. Drye graciously invited us to stay at his home on Sunday night and speak to his team and students at the school the following Monday morning.

When we showed up that Sunday night, we quickly realized our dad had seriously underplayed Mr. Drye's success. The enormity of his house and property made it clear he had experienced financial success beyond anything we'd ever seen.

As we gaped in amazement, we could tell what we both were thinking—*What kind of business does this guy have, and how can we get involved?*

Mr. Drye showed us to our room and told us to be ready by 7 a.m. the following day. As we lay there in the darkened silence of that room, we quietly marveled at how successful this man was. We didn't run in circles with people like this.

We drifted off to sleep in the amazing beds, the comfort of which far exceeded the twin-sized mattresses in our Liberty dorm room. Then, at 4:30 a.m., we were startled awake by someone yelling down the hall.

Jumping out of bed, we both got up and crept to the door. Cracking it open, we peered down the long, dark hallway. We could see light coming out from under the door of Mr. Drye's office. As we stood there with hearts pounding, we realized he wasn't yelling—he was praying!

For the next hour, we heard him pour his heart out to the Lord and do battle with the enemy. He would go from telling God how much he loved Him to rebuking the devil in the name of Jesus. "You have no authority over my family or my business, Devil!" he shouted. "Get away from them!"

We had grown up in a family that believed in prayer and put that belief into practice. But this was a whole new level— never before had we seen such emphatic prayer. This man sounded like he was locked in a hand-to-hand combat with the devil.

Fortunately, we were able to fall back asleep for about an hour. Then we crawled out of bed, washed up, and headed downstairs to talk to our newfound prayer warrior/business tycoon buddy.

"We heard you praying early this morning," we told Mr. Drye.

"Oh. Sorry about that," he said. "I go to war on my knees before I start my day, or I don't feel right."

After breakfast, we were whisked away in his Suburban to his office, where we were to speak to his staff. On the way, we asked him how he started his business.

"I began in insurance," he said. "But then I realized I wanted to create something that could make millions of dollars to fund God's work on the earth. So I got into real estate."

Whoa. We had never heard anyone talk like that before. A person who wanted to make millions of dollars to give away!?

Before asking any further questions, we pulled up to a big white building with the words "David Drye Company" on the marquee. We walked into the foyer and up the stairs to a large conference room where about thirty people were gathered, waiting for Mr. Drye—and us.

We thought *This guy has thirty employees? That's huge!* We were impressed, but then we found out these were only a few of his leaders and support staff. His company employed over four hundred people, who managed his forty-three apartment complexes across three states.

We spent the whole day with Mr. Drye, hauling us from one speaking engagement to the next. The longer we were with him, the more impressed and inspired we became. We asked him no fewer than 100 questions. We couldn't drive more than two or three miles without him pointing out another apartment complex he owned, a fun park he had opened, or an office complex he had built.

He explained that his entire business was built upon prayer the whole time. "I have prayed for the last twenty years that God would bless my business," he said. "I shout, '*God, bust those rocks and break those chains that hold back Your blessing from me. I commit my way to You. Give me more that I may bless You with it!*'

Then he looked at us with a big grin and said, "Boys, God has answered those prayers."

While he was talking, his fists were balled up and swinging wildly. He was a very passionate guy. And he had no idea how to wait until his truck came to a complete stop before he changed gears. He'd back out of a parking spot at warp speed and slam it into drive before he even pushed the brake. It was an adventurous ride that day—in more ways than one.

At the end of the day, as we were driving back to his house, he asked if we would mind flying back to Liberty in his helicopter since he didn't have time to drive us back.

Ummm, are you kidding? We thought. *That might just make us the most popular dudes at LU!* We had never been in a helicopter before.

When we pulled onto the half-mile-long driveway leading to his house, Mr. Drye reached into his pocket and pulled out a small, worn piece of paper. "Do you boys know what this is?" he asked.

"No, sir," we answered.

"On this sheet of paper," he continued, "I've written goals for my family and business. When you guys heard me this morning, I was laying my hands on these goals and asking God to help me accomplish everything on the list. But I know Satan doesn't want me to succeed, so when I pray, I know I've entered a battlefield in the spiritual realm. I wage war in the spirit before I go to war in business."

As he was talking, he handed us the piece of paper.

"Take a look," he said. "I want you to see what I've written on there. I don't usually do this, but I feel the Lord wants me to let you see it."

We couldn't get past the first point: *Give away $1 million a month.*

We had never seen a number like that before, much less seen it written down as a specific goal and prayed over by a man well on his way to accomplishing it.

He looked at us with penetrating eyes. "Boys, I believe God has a great plan for both of you. But that plan will only go as far as your prayer life is deep. You need to go after God in prayer like never before. Make big goals for yourselves, spiritually and financially, and then go after them until He either grants your request or gives you something else to ask for."

When we handed the paper back to him, he asked us something unexpected. "When baseball is over, would you consider coming to work for me? I've been praying for God to spark a revival in America right here from Concord, and I want to pour myself into young men like you, teaching you everything I know."

Uh, do bears poop in the woods? We responded with an emphatic "*Yes!*"

David Drye gave us a vision for life after baseball: to be part of a thriving company led by a man who wanted to change the world for Christ.

Just before we left, he opened the back door of his Suburban, reached into one of several boxes inside, and handed us each a copy of *The Autobiography of George Müller*.

"Aside from the Bible, this is the best book I've ever read," he told us. "I give them out to everyone I can. I have modeled my prayer life after this great man, and you should too."

Müller's claim to fame was that he built an orphanage in England in the 1800s solely through the power of prayer. He committed to never asking anyone for money to help with his projects; when he needed funds, he would ask God alone. His little orphanage, which started with just a few orphans in one house, grew to thousands in a sprawling campus of houses—all because he partnered with God to meet his needs.

Inside each book was Mr. Drye's business card. The front of the card simply read "*Jesus Loves You*" in big red letters, and his contact information was on the back. This was a simple way for him to let people know what was most important in his life.

We prayed together and then said goodbye.

Our heads were buzzing on the flight back to Liberty—not just because we were stoked to be flying in a helicopter but because we felt our future had just opened up for us in a way neither of us had foreseen.

That day transformed not only our prayer lives but also our understanding of money. Mr. Drye showed us the powerful connection between the two—how his prayers fueled his financial success and how that success, in turn, gave him the freedom to devote even more time to prayer.

We also read the book by Müller. It's a must-read for anyone who wants God as a financial advisor.

A year later, we were drafted into professional baseball. I (Jason) was in my second year as a minor leaguer for the Orioles when I broke my leg in Hickory, North Carolina, less than an hour from where Mr. Drye lived. We tell the details in our book *Miracle in Shreveport*. It was an epic break that required emergency surgery and several days in the hospital.

Because it was the final game of a seven-day road trip, our team couldn't wait for me, so they left me behind and headed home. By the time I got out of surgery, I was stuck in Hickory, alone in a hospital room.

The following day, after I finished breakfast, I heard a knock at the door. "Come in," I called, wondering who it could be. To my total amazement, it was David Drye and one of his sons. We hadn't seen each other in two years.

He stepped into the hospital room. "We heard about what happened to you, and we came to pray for your healing," he said as a huge smile crossed his face. "You didn't think you could be so close to us, and I wouldn't come see you, did you?"

"How did you hear?" I asked.

"Your dad called last night to ask for prayer," Mr Drye responded. "So I told him I would do even better—I'd come pray for you in person."

I was thankful to see a familiar face, and I was even more grateful that it was a man who prayed like him.

As we talked, he handed out his "*Jesus Loves You*" business card to every nurse and doctor who entered the room. Before leaving, he tucked one into the picture frame on the wall by my bed. Every day I spent in that hospital, I looked at that card and thanked God for a man like David Drye.

After we prayed together, I said, "I just gotta ask—did you fly your helicopter here?"

He flashed that grin once again. "Yep. Landed it on the roof."

He then asked if I'd read the book on George Müller. I told him I had and that it was worth the recommendation. He said he'd send me a case full of them so I could give them to the guys on my team.

"Don't forget," he said as he and his son got up to leave, "I want you and David to move to Concord and work with me when baseball is over."

"That's a deal," I said.

He leaned over and hugged me. After he left the room, I was struck with the feeling that this was one of the greatest human beings I had ever met. I remember thinking it would be nice to be like him one day.

One month later, I was recovering at my parents' house in Dallas when we got a phone call.

"David Drye and his wife, Ann, were just killed in a plane crash," said the voice on the other end of the line.

I lost my breath.

They had been traveling in his private plane, headed to their beach house, when one of the engines failed. The pilot almost made it back to the runway, but their wing clipped a tree, and the plane flipped upside down. No one survived.

I couldn't wrap my head around what I was hearing. It just didn't seem possible—how could he be gone? My mind raced in a hundred directions at once. I had placed so much hope in a future with Mr. Drye, learning how to run a business grounded in biblical principles and how to live out radical generosity with money. And now, in an instant, he was gone.

Two days later, while I was still in shock from that phone call, I received a package from Concord. I opened it, and there was the case of George Müller books Mr. Drye had promised to send. On top was a scribbled note in his handwriting:

"Have fun giving these out. Let's talk soon—David Drye."

Tears filled my eyes, and I fought hard to keep it together. That box had been mailed to me before he boarded the plane that day. One of his final acts on this earth was sending me a collection of faith-building books—tools to share the testimony of a man who lived by faith, partnered with God to provide his every need, and inspired others to do the same.

I placed one of the copies on my bookshelf. I still have it today. It serves as a constant reminder, not just of the prayer-warrior minister the book is about but also of the prayer-warrior businessman who gave it to me. He modeled what true success means.

Two years later, in 2001, when my baseball career came to an end, my wife and I moved to Concord, NC, where I stepped into the role of ministry coordinator for the David Drye Company. It was a position Mr. Drye created before his passing, with a three-fold mission: to serve as chaplain for the employees, outreach coordinator for the community, and donation manager for the company's monthly giving.

The following year, in 2002, David wrapped up his baseball career and moved his young family to Concord, where he took a job as the janitor at the school founded by Mr. Drye. By the end of that year, the rest of our family followed— Mom, Dad, our brother and two sisters, and their families— all relocating to Concord.

In January 2003, we took the leap and launched our own venture into business. With Mr. Drye's legacy as our guide, we built that first company on Biblical principles, saturated every step in prayer, and committed to radical generosity. And in the words of the man who inspired it all, "God has answered those prayers!"

ENDNOTES

1   Penny Lea, *Sing A Little Louder,* http://www.
    internationalwallofprayer.org/A-010-Holocaust-Memorial-
    Day-Stover.html

2   Goodreads.com

3   Dr. Tony Evans, *Kingdom Agenda*

4   Dictionary.com

5   Tony Evans, *Kingdom Agenda*

6   Visit LoveLife.org for more information.

7   https://compassfinancialministry.org/wp-content/
    uploads/2024/04/2350-Verses-Catalog.pdf

8   https://biblehub.com/hebrew/3925.htm

9   https://biblehub.com/hebrew/3276.htm

10 Dictionary.com

11 Dictionary.com

12 https://tonycooke.org/articles-by-tony-cooke/rivers-of-eden/

13 As we said before, "...so long as you live in a free country
    where economic prosperity is an option."

14 Robert Fraser, in *Marketplace Christianity: Discovering the Kingdom Purpose of the Marketplace* (Oasis House, 2004), first shared the concept.

15 Oswald Chambers - *My Utmost For His Highest*

16 Logos Bible word study

17 We wrote a book titled Bold & Broken: *Becoming The Bridge Between Heaven & Earth* - visit BenhamBrothers.com for more info

18 https://quotefancy.co

19 Walter Mischel, *The Marshmallow Test: Why Self Control Is the Engine of Success* (Little, Brown and Company, 2015).

20 Timothy Keller, quoted by Amy Sherman in her book *Kingdom Calling*